READING FOR ACTION

READING FOR ACTION

Engaging Youth in Social Justice through Young Adult Literature

Ashley S. Boyd and Janine J. Darragh

ROWMAN & LITTLEFIELD
Lanham • Boulder • New York • London

Published by Rowman & Littlefield
An imprint of The Rowman & Littlefield Publishing Group, Inc.
4501 Forbes Boulevard, Suite 200, Lanham, Maryland 20706
www.rowman.com

6 Tinworth Street, London SE11 5AL

British Library Cataloguing in Publication Information Available

Library of Congress Cataloging-in-Publication Data Available

ISBN: 978-1-4758-4666-9 (cloth : alk. paper)
ISBN: 978-1-4758-4667-6 (pbk. : alk. paper)
ISBN: 978-1-4758-4668-3 (electronic)

♾ ™ The paper used in this publication meets the minimum requirements of American National Standard for Information Sciences—Permanence of Paper for Printed Library Materials, ANSI/NISO Z39.48-1992.

Printed in the United States of America

CONTENTS

FOREWORD

Young adult literature has been a trojan horse, a large body of transformative stories secreted into the curriculum to open windows and doors, small and large; the friend we always wanted even if/when we did not know we wanted her/him/them; the families we have not had and/or enhanced the families we are a part of and the families we can be a part of, even if not in the same household or community, near or far; an elixir; a gateway drug to the classics; a transport to other worlds; a safe haven. Young adult literature has been a shield, a cudgel, a mirror; a prolific world maker, generating rich and round characters who tell stories upon stories of the many, for the many, rather than the few, stories that create and recreate new bodies and ways of being.

We have tapped young adult literature to hoist on its many shoulders myriad causes: to improve reading comprehension; to increase motivation to read literature, fiction and non-fiction; to help students understand and confront bullying; to learn about and empathize with those living with mental health issues, their own and/or their loved ones; to unpack the complexities of people in poverty, pushing back against pervasive stereotypes; to challenge the gender binary and heteronormativity and construct more inclusive gender and sexual identities; to depict the costs of systems of oppression upon people of color, providing opportunities for students and teachers to engage in an array of social justice literacies with which, together, they can begin to work toward change at any level possible; and, simply, to provide fascinating reads for adolescents (and for those of us who are a wee bit older). Surely no one can say young adult literature has been hesitant to explore the confounding issues of our time.

Reading for Action: Engaging Youth in Social Justice through Young Adult Literature, however, suggests that young adult literature can do even more. Freire and Macedo (1987) argued that "if the texts generally offered students once hid much more than they revealed of reality, now literacy as an act of knowledge, as a creative act and as a political act, is an effort to read the world and the word. Now it is no longer possible to have the text without context" (p. 43). Book by timely book, contextualizing and interrogating the issues in our world within which inequities are produced, walls built and bolstered, systemic obstacles thrown up to deny individuals the individuality we as a country purportedly believe is one of our core values, *Reading for Action* shouts out that what we do in our classes need not and should not stay in the classroom.

Friere and Macedo (1987) also maintained that "the educational space reproduces the dominant ideology. However, it is possible within educational institutions to contradict imposed dominant values" (p. 126). Though I do not think Boyd and Darragh ever use the word "revolution," they have indeed mapped a fully-strategized curricular revolution for the English Language Arts classroom. Beginning with a selection of compelling young adult literature texts about current social topics, modeling the kind of critical dialogue that should be the lifeblood of our classrooms, each chapter then posits the kinds of actions that can begin to tear down barriers, act by determined act. *Reading for Action* is a project brimming with resistance/s to and disruptions of the status quo.

The preservice and early-career teachers I have the honor to work with frequently comment that they are overwhelmed with all they need to accomplish with students in their classrooms in the midst of events occurring in the world today, careful and caring pedagogy and curriculum awash in the wake of mass shootings in schools and other public spaces; extreme weather bringing more and more uncertainty to the future world of their prospective students; a rapidly changing economy raising questions about how their students can make a path in their life; and political systems locally and nationally that exacerbate rather than mitigate the problems that cause unrelenting suffering for far too many. Greene (1995) recognized that anxiety, writing that "There is no question but that some students face fearful obstacles due to the inequities in this country" (p. 18). She believed, as a result, "that a general inability to conceive a better order of things can give rise to resignation that paralyzes and prevents people from acting to bring about change" (pp. 18–19). But Greene was not one to acquiesce. She pointed out that, "We also have our social imagination: the capacity to invent visions of what should be and what might be in our deficient society, on the streets where we live, in our schools" (p. 5).

As we are surrounded by the towering, toppling issues and events that trouble our lives, our instinct may be to run. But *Reading for Action* shows us that we can stand our ground, take a breath, look each other in the eyes, roll up our sleeves, and together envision ways to chip away at these precarious towers, to move forward, to imagine and create safe spaces within which to effect significant change. *Reading for Action* will be a guide for teachers who want to make a difference with their students not only in the classroom, students acquiring critical skills, content knowledge, and cultural understanding, but also in their day-to-day lives in their communities beyond school. It is about time for a book like this founded on close reading of contemporary young adult literature, steeped in deep understandings of critical pedagogies. I think we are more than ready for it.

—Crag Hill, Associate Professor, The University of Oklahoma

REFERENCES

Freire, P., & Macedo, D. P. (1987). *Literacy: Reading the word & the world*. London: Routledge & Kegan Paul.

Greene, M. (1995). *Releasing the imagination: Essays on education, the arts, and social change*. San Francisco: Jossey-Bass Publishers.

PREFACE

This book came about as the result of numerous conversations between the two of us about young adult literature, teachers, and social justice. We love our work, our students, and young adult texts, and we are both passionate about issues of equity and society. We knew that these areas could and should be combined, yet both of us—former secondary English teachers—also know too well the struggle that teachers often face: the desperate desire to implement a new lesson or unit combined with the sheer lack of time to invest in researching and locating appropriate resources and texts. Teachers' attention is often pulled in what feels like a million directions with the pressures of testing and paperwork, responding to students' individual needs and parents' concerns, and working with colleagues and administrators.

We strongly feel, however, that the majority of teachers also support the fight for a better society and the disruption of inequity, that they see poverty, racism, and sexism in our world and in their daily lives at school. Yet we also know that, in addition to the time constraints and pressures just mentioned, approaching oft-considered controversial topics and taking action with students can been intimidating. We hoped that if we could provide not only practicing teachers but also our preservice candidates (who experience similar anxieties regarding their future careers) with a comprehensive resource that offered young adult texts matched with social problems and myriad ideas for teaching those texts and encouraging students' action, we might be able to paint a portrait of the kind of teaching we envision and assist teachers in designing curriculum that engenders change. Thus, this book was born.

ACKNOWLEDGMENTS

I, Ashley, want to thank first and foremost my coauthor, friend, colleague, writing buddy, running mentor, healthy-eating companion (ha!), and fellow unsweet tea drinker, Janine Darragh. You jumped on board whole-heartedly with this project and never looked back. It is because of you it came to fruition. Thank you for keeping us moving, holding to deadlines, and being an all-around wonderful person with whom to work. I truly cannot say enough what a pleasure it has been to write this with you, and I look forward to many more projects!

To my colleagues in the English department at WSU and across campus, I am grateful for your support and mentorship. To my friends, near and far, who listen and encourage and show up for the big and small successes and sympathize with setbacks, thank you. To my family, both in the Carolinas and in Washington, thank you for your constant support and encouragement. And especially to my mom, who lives every day of the writing process with me and never tires, thank you for listening and being my biggest cheerleader. Finally, to Keith, thank you for your unwavering love, care, and encouragement. I am ever grateful for your patience, humor, wisdom, and feedback, and I appreciate you more than words can express.

On April 3, 2018, Ashley Boyd sent me (Janine Darragh) a text that read: "Hey friend! Want to write a book about using YA literature to inspire social action projects?" Eight months later, that simple text morphed into this book. I can't thank Ashley enough for inviting me to join her with this project, leading the way through the process and enthusiastically supporting every suggestion and answering every question I had along the way.

I also want to thank my parents, Dan and Lynn Darragh, who have always nurtured my love of writing and words and are true examples and my personal role models for social action in their own community. Thanks to my Ohio family (Debbie, David, Becca, Brendan, Jared, Maryanne) and friends and colleagues in Idaho, Ohio, and Washington, who have been supportive throughout the process, especially Kendra, my sounding board, exercise partner, and biggest cheerleader, and my TA, Jill—without her assistance this book would not have been completed by the deadline. A special thank you to Greg, who not only patiently listened to me talk about this project over the past eight months but also watched countless documentaries, listened to audio books, and went to museums with me in support of the research I was doing on various chapters. I appreciate your support, care, kindness, and willingness to always get a cheeseburger when one was desperately needed. You keep me steady and balanced. Thank you. So very much.

To the Fall 2018 students of Washington State University's Engl 325 and University of Idaho's EDCI 404 Young Adult literature courses, thank you for reading and analyzing the books included in this project, piloting the activities, and developing your own social action projects. Your enthusiasm, feedback, laughter, critique, and belief in this book were invaluable to us. You all impressed us every day, and your own action projects showed us that what we suggest in this book is not only possible but is necessary, and that when left to design their own civic endeavors, students' creations extend beyond what we can even imagine. It is amazing humans like you, who are training to be English teachers, who make us so optimistic about the future—of education and of our country.

Finally, thank you to all the teachers and young adults who are eager to shine their light into the world and to make it just a little bit better for those around them. You inspire us every day. This book is for you.

INTRODUCTION

The world is an increasingly complex place, and the complicated nature of society, documented through social media, news outlets, and popular culture, is a part of youths' daily realities. It is imperative that teachers work with the students in their classrooms to understand, unpack, and address the pressing social issues that they routinely encounter. With various competing sources for attention, teachers can provide spaces for students to navigate the social issues of their era and to cultivate the myriad literacies required for them to read their worlds critically, understand and respond intellectually, and act upon their environments.

Young people are ready to speak up and act. This is evidenced, for example, by the number of youths raising their voices in the wake of school shootings, joining campaigns against police brutality, or marching in protest for women's rights. Often, however, such efforts are made by small factions of impassioned students and take place outside of classrooms, on their own time and by those with access to such outlets. Teens need knowledge about the avenues available for taking action as well as support and guidance for doing so. Teachers can play vital roles in teaching youths about social action and engaging them in organized efforts. In this book, we posit that secondary English teachers in particular can welcome social issues into their classrooms and facilitate youth civic action, and we suggest young adult literature as one medium through which such work can occur.

We assert the importance of developing students' responses to cultural matters from their current status, *as teens*, so that they begin to develop agency and can discern their capacity for making a difference in the world. Too often, teens are prepared for a distant future or made to feel, once they have fostered their critical capacities, that nothing can be done because they are too young (Boyd, 2017), and they are left feeling hopeless (Downey, 2005). This book proposes a multitude of ways that teachers can encourage students to read and act in the moment. It is, of course, our hope that this will produce students who carry equity-related work over into their adult lives as participants in our democracy, but our focus here is on the readers present within the secondary classroom space.

YOUNG ADULT LITERATURE: THE GROWTH OF A FIELD

To set the stage for the type of literature to which we will refer in this text, it is necessary to define and trace, briefly, the history of young adult literature and the rise of the field. We utilize Nilsen and Donelson's (2012) criteria to define young adult literature as texts written specifically for young adults, individuals ranging approximately age twelve to eighteen. These works for youths are generally characterized by their first-person point of view (from that of a teen), fast-paced plots, and focus on the resiliency and independence of teens. They cover a variety of genres, including but certainly not limited to romance, and deal with topics and emotions that teens find appealing or are experiencing themselves, such as loss, the search for identity, and bullying. Young adult literature "also implicitly or explicitly challenge[s] the dominant assumptions contemporary culture conveys to adolescents" (Hill, 2014, p. 8). Works in this field can assume various formats including prose, verse, audiobooks, and graphic novels (Butcher & Hinton, 2013).

Scholars who chart the development of young adult literature over time generally begin in the 1960s with the publication of works such as *The Outsiders* (Hinton, 1967), characterized by its realistic portrayal of class warfare in America from the perspective of the teens affected. The 1970s, the "first golden age" of young adult literature (Cart, 2010, p. 31), witnessed the publication of Robert Cormier's (1974) *The Chocolate War*, a novel that proffered that "not all endings of novels and real lives are happy ones" (Cart, 2010, p. 30), thereby opening the door for authors to come. The 1980s young adult literature was reflected in romance series books like *Sweet Valley High* (Pascal, 1986), as well as horror books such as R. L. Stine's *Fear Street* (1989). Critiqued, however, for their focus on mainstream, White, middle-class characters at a time when immigrant populations were rising, in the 1990s "books began to reflect the interactivity and connectivity of the digital world with shifting perspectives, diverse voices, and even multiple genres within a single book" (Butcher & Hinton, 2013, p. 6). The field hit a lull in the early 1990s but experienced a reawakening in the latter half of the decade as teen populations rose in numbers. Authors became committed to authentic portrayals of teens, and young adult literature as a field became distinct from children's literature (Cart, 2010), and thus was taken more seriously.

In more recent decades, young adult authors have gained widespread popularity and readers have become more sophisticated, resulting in a vast array of new texts within the field. As a whole, these latest texts are more inclusive, especially in terms of points of view and reflecting protagonists from different ethnicities, social classes, and sexualities. This shift reflects more changes in the population of the United States at large, as the diversity in ethnicities has continued to rise and the spectrum of gender and sexuality becomes increasingly recognized.

For instance, authors who are Latinx (e.g., Meg Medina) and African American (e.g., Jason Reynolds) have begun to integrate their own experiences from their youth into their novels, and there is a growing body of work that addresses lesbian, gay, bisexual, transgender, queer, intersex, and asexual (LGBTQIA) communities. There has especially been a rise in works specific to individuals who identify as transgender (e.g., Gold, 2012). While once considered "too White" (Larrick, 1965), literature for children and young adults is thus evolving. Students, other than traditional, White, middle-class youth, are now able to find themselves in texts, and students from dominant groups are able to learn about cultures and histories outside of their own in powerful ways—through personalized narratives with exciting plots, familiar language, and complex themes.

Despite these advances, as Hill (2014) writes, "YA literature has come a long way, but it has a long way to go" (p. 3). Cart (2010) reports that of three thousand books:

> In 2008 a grand total of 389 books were published to give faces to how many tens of millions of young people who have been—and still are— regarded as "the other." The situation is even worse if you limit the number of books to those created by authors and artists working from within the culture. (p. 126)

And Toliver (2018), recounting data from the Cooperative Children's Book Center (CCBC), notes, in the "number of books written by and about Black people between 2002 and 2017 . . . no more than 3.5% of the total number of children's books are written by Black authors and feature Black characters" (p. 11). Toliver illustrates, too, how specific representations of Black female protagonists are privileged in the texts that are published, often excluding narratives that, for example, include science fiction and fantasy. She rightfully argues, "Black girls need access to stories depicting racism, prejudice, and realism alongside narratives that portray hope, imagination, and diverse futures" (pp. 18–19). Expanding the representation of diverse youths and widespread availability of texts portraying those youths therefore continues to be crucial in the field.

While publishing companies have been criticized for the lack of multicultural books for young adults, they have responded by emphasizing a lack of demand for such works and thereby a problem with profit. Although a situation thus riddled with conflicts, regardless of these, youths need access to books that not only reflect themselves but also teach about cultures aside from their own and represent individuals with lives unlike their own. In response to this dearth in the field, in 2014 the #weneed diversebooks (WNDB) campaign was "created to address the lack of diverse, non-majority narratives in children's literature. WNDB is committed to the ideal that embracing diversity will lead to acceptance, empathy, and ultimately equality" (2018, para. 1). The organization boasts a number of programs, grants, and partnerships to recognize and distribute more multicultural literature. Thus, efforts are underway to address this concern in the field, and inclusive texts, as shared above, are on the rise. In this book, we draw upon many of these texts, suggesting their value in classrooms and potential to not only reflect students but also to incite them to take action.

THE BENEFITS OF READING YOUNG ADULT LITERATURE

In addition to authors in the field of young adult literature, scholars in academia have also written extensively *about* young adult texts, documenting their many benefits. Among other advantages, teachers have utilized young adult literature "to help address remedial and reluctant readers; to teach literary elements; to encourage multiculturalism; to create bridges to the classics; to introduce different literary theories; to promote the acceptance of differences; as the basis for interdisciplinary curriculum" (Hill, 2014, p. 9). This list continues to grow as the field gains more diverse texts that allow students to read from different perspectives.

Perhaps one of the most extensive qualitative studies on the use of young adult literature to date is Ivey and Johnston's (2013), with data from seventy-one student interviews and classroom observations. The researchers found a number of positive outcomes associated with young adults reading texts written for them. Most notable were results related to student engagement, evidenced by students "reading for extended periods within and outside of school and beyond sanctioned times" (p. 260) as well as outcomes such as: a growth in peer relationships centered on reading books, shifts in student identities as readers, and stronger senses of agency in academics *and* in life narratives. In addition, their study found that students in the focal classes who read young adult literature throughout the year experienced increased test scores. For example, "The pass rate for the economically disadvantaged group went from 69% to 81%" (p. 266). While some worry that young adult literature will not aid students in acquiring the skills needed for standardized tests, this study clearly shows the opposite.

Others (Glaus, 2014; Miller, 2014) have validated, in fact, how young adult literature can achieve many of the professional standards to which teachers are beholden, such as the Common Core State Standards (CCSS). When examining texts qualitatively through the lens of text complexity, as Glaus (2014) demonstrates, young adult literature provides the "unconventional structures, varying levels of meaning, and varying levels of clarity for readers" that would score highly on the measures used in the CCSS. Comparable, then, to traditional works, young adult literature is sufficiently sophisticated and can challenge students.

Miller (2014) cautions against the notion that all young adult literature meets advanced criteria, however, and developed a nuanced rubric to assist teachers in choosing texts that meet the criteria, especially for use in accelerated and advanced placement courses. The point, however, not to be lost, is that *adolescent texts can achieve the standards required even in the most advanced classes*. Furthermore, even as an emphasis on informational texts soars in secondary curriculum, young adult literature has proven to meet the occasion (Hayn, Kaplan, Nolen, & Olvey, 2015). For example, Boyd and Dyches (2017) show how a nonfiction text, *Enrique's Journey* (Nazario, 2014), prompted students to cultivate their reading skills related to point of view, visual literacy, and style while simultaneously complicating their perspectives on immigration. Darragh and Radmer's (2016) work also demonstrated that students reading young adult literature performed just as well as their peers who read only the course textbook on an end-of-year standardized test.

The multiple potential outcomes of reading young adult literature, its ability to satisfy standards and move beyond them to recognitions of humanity, are critical. Most relevant to this book, young adult literature has the power to serve as both a window and a mirror (Bishop, 1990), an argument made consistently throughout the declarations of its benefits in classrooms. In reflecting students who are often marginalized in traditional curriculum, such as those along the gender spectrum or of race and ethnicities other than the often-presented White European American, this body of literature can empower students to imagine futures that they may otherwise not have seen themselves accomplishing. It can validate their experiences, showing that they are not alone in the world, and it can encourage them to speak up for even more representation. In facilitating awareness, acceptance, and inclusion of others, young adult literature can ignite the development of empathy and compassion for people whose realities are different from the reader (Boyd & Bereiter, 2017; Cartledge, Gardner, & Ford, 2009; Freeman & Lehman, 2001; Kurkjian & Livingston, 2007; Rosenblatt, 1933/1995; Soter, 1999). Through identifying with powerful, first-person narratives, doors can open for students that simple historical, factual, or even often media-based accounts cannot accomplish.

YOUNG ADULT LITERATURE AND CONTROVERSIAL ISSUES

In addition to the growth of diverse authors in young adult literature as well as to its empirical benefits in classrooms and ability to achieve professional standards, the content of young adult literature reflects oft-considered controversial topics, mirroring cultural themes such as justice and mental health. Issues that have been treated as taboo by society are tackled directly in young adult literature and can therefore be powerful avenues for student learning. These include topics such as rape (e.g., Anderson, 1999), religion (e.g., Jones, 2011), and depression (e.g., Green & Levithan, 2011). Exposure to these themes at such pivotal points in students' lives affords an opportunity for adolescent readers to begin to develop their own thoughts and perspectives on a subject that may be affecting their friends and/or themselves and to seek out additional information.

The ability of young adult literature to cultivate students' understandings of a multitude of cultural topics has been well documented. Students who read, for example, *Enrique's Journey* (Nazario, 2014) have noted their better understanding of issues surrounding immigration and were able to better discern those individuals who leave their home countries to escape poverty and abuse in additive rather than deficit frameworks (Boyd & Dyches, 2017). Students who read *Stuck in Neutral* (Trueman, 2000), a book with a character with cerebral palsy, reported higher intentions to interact recreationally and socially with individuals with disabilities (Darragh, 2015). While disabilities at first may not seem a controversial issue, representations of disabilities as well as society's response to individuals are continued areas of struggle in both academic literature and popular discourse. Teachers, too, have worked against homophobia through their own reading of young adult literature (Clark & Blackburn, 2009), and youth reading books with transgender protagonists have been better able to understand the gender spectrum (Boyd & Bereiter, 2017). These are all issues that teens hear about daily on the news, at home, among their peers, or may even be aspects that affect them personally.

And yet, despite the prevalence of these issues in the lives of teens, censorship of them abounds from parents and educational stakeholders who wish to protect their children. Seeking to avoid issues such as racism, violence, or profanity (Curry, 2001), parents often challenge the existence of books in schools and classroom curriculum that reflect those elements. With its emphasis on reality, of which these controversial elements are inextricable, young adult literature is prone to censorship. In fact, young adult literature often appears in the top ten most frequently challenged and banned book lists, such as those issued each year by the American Library Association.

In 2017, for example, three of the top ten included young adult titles. Teens, however, admit that they already know much of the content deemed inappropriate for them (Denzin, 2013). As Cart (2010) writes,

"One certainly understands and empathizes with parents and other concerned adults who wish to protect youngsters from the sensationalistic,
the meretricious, and the mendacious . . . and . . . parents need to be aware
of and responsible for their offspring's reading, viewing, and interacting
habits" (p. 162). Yet if teachers and parents exclude material from their
classrooms that asks students to think critically about their worlds, they
are ignoring an opportunity to help them navigate complicated topics in
an intellectual space or, worse even, are ignoring intellectualism altogether.

Young adult literature is a medium through which controversial issues
can be explored and sides weighed via the first-person narratives of those
affected by the issues at hand. Ellen Wittlinger, author of the novel *Par-
rotfish*, which contains a transgender protagonist, shared in her keynote
address at the 2012 Massachusetts Library Association Teen Summit,
"Once you know someone personally, your prejudices fall away" (Sokoll,
2013, p. 24). If books are conduits through which readers can "get to
know someone" and young adult literature especially accomplishes this
goal for teens, then students might get to know someone who relates to a
larger culture issue. From that learning, they be more likely to engage
with the topic in a productive way. By humanizing the controversies of
our era, young adult literature invites readers to understand. From there,
we invite readers to act.

SOCIAL ACTION AND YOUNG ADULT LITERATURE: A NEW CONDUIT

The idea of leading youth to social action has been broadly conceived of
in classrooms, especially those devoted to learning about civics and social
studies and even some focused on a critical English Language Arts (Morrell, 2005). Yet, while young adult literature addresses controversial issues and develops students' greater understandings of topics such as gender inequity or social class disparities, the leap from *understanding* to
action using such texts is lesser imagined. In the chapters to come, we
intend to bridge that gap by illustrating how young adult literature can be
a catalyst for social action and through offering a plethora of examples
for educators.

As Epstein (2013) explains, social action projects are "a type of civic education" that "provide opportunities for individuals to critically assess the social landscape around them and then address identified injustices by taking concrete action steps" (p. 125). A spectrum of social action exists (Boyd, 2017; Canadian Teachers' Federation, 2010) from direct action, in which participants actually make change themselves to indirect action, in which they influence those with the actual power to make change. For example, contacting policymakers via letter writing and phone campaigns to sway their perspective on immigration is an example of indirect action, while implementing an effort to reinvigorate and clean a local park for children's use is direct action. Simmons (2012) detailed how *The Hunger Games* could easily lead to an examination of hunger in America, involuntary labor, and the sex trade. Glasgow (2001) outlines how specific young adult texts address forms of oppression such as those that are built around race, disability, and sexual orientation. Finally, Bomer and Bomer (2001) have solidified how social action involves literacy skills of reading, writing, and processing information. And Boyd (2017) argues that through an expanded notion of literacy as a social practice (Gee, 2015), social action projects allow students to learn new discourses or ways of being as they assume the persona of an activist and negotiate themselves with assorted actors of differing power differentials.

Generally, and it is vital to note, action projects cultivate students' interests or concerns and "allow students to express their feelings and desire for change" (Simmons, 2012, p. 25). Thus, the importance of student agency in the work we suggest cannot be overstated. Social action projects, if they are to be successful, must stem from issues with which students are concerned, and students must be instrumental in labeling the problem they see and determining the steps to take toward addressing it. Teachers should guide the processes that students develop, monitor their progress, and offer lessons as needed along the way (Bomer & Bomer, 2001; Boyd, 2017), but youth are the ultimate actors. This process, when incorporated into the classroom space as an integral part of daily instruction and activity, can better prepare students to become democratic citizens in their society (Epstein, 2014). It can teach them that they are capable of making change, even as youth, and it can help them discern the processes by which such change happens.

OVERVIEW OF BOOK

Hill (2014), in his call for a concerted effort in the field around uses of young adult literature, states, "We must . . . continue to provide resources for secondary teachers (lesson ideas, rationales for texts, bibliographies of novels, critical commentary)" (p. 8). This book answers that call by illustrating, through specific textual examples and teaching strategies, how literature written for young adult audiences reflects current social topics and how educators can build on these works to incite students to civic action. Our approach is therefore unique not only in how we meld the two fields but also in our attention to the practical aspects of teaching combined with theoretical perspectives on cultural issues.

In what remains, we focus on twelve contemporary social issues identified by professional educational organizations (e.g., NCTE, CEE, NEA) and teens as currently pressing: bullying, global poverty, supports for mental health, the gender spectrum, human trafficking, the refugee crisis, women's rights, social class disparities in the United States, police brutality, immigration reform, sexual orientations and stigmas, and ecojustice and environmental protection. We recognize that the issues in this text do not exist in isolation and that areas of oppression intersect (Crenshaw, 1989), and we emphasize this notion in each chapter.

Yet ultimately, we believe that foregrounding each topic in this way provides an accessible text for both teachers and students and a way to begin the critical conversations we believe are essential to classrooms. Furthermore, we are fully aware that there are additional areas of oppression and controversy reflected in society. We concentrate on those we do because of their prevalence in the current social milieu and due to our desire to engage students with those themes that they have identified as important issues that plague society. We conceptualize these specifically as controversial social issues, rather than merely loosely as topics such as *racism* or *gender* to ensure that they reflect identifiable matters that can— and need to be—addressed and to make explicit the actual tangible *problem* at hand. In doing this also we are able to locate pragmatic actions for students and teachers that actually address the theme and work toward change.

We devote one chapter to each of these social issues, and in each provide an overview of the problem, noting briefly its history and manifestations. Then, we offer a work from young adult literature that illustrates the issue through an affected protagonist or storyline in which this is a central concern. Our descriptions of the texts may contain spoilers, as we feel holistic overviews of the texts are required for teachers to choose judiciously which ones they may want to implement in their classrooms. We then move into teaching strategies, offering before, during, and after reading ideas for relating to the text and understanding the social topic, and we provide suggestions for social action projects and avenues for student research and exploration. We conclude each chapter with proposed canonical companions and additional young adult literature surrounding the same theme and also include related media in the form of popular songs. As the topics we address are serious social issues, the resources we include reflect that same gravity, and thus we recommend that teachers screen all suggestions and determine their appropriateness for their individual contexts.

As noted above, it is key for teachers to remember that social action must ultimately be student driven. Therefore, what we hope to offer in this book are ideas and recommendations for teachers hoping to utilize texts for social justice. They are only *potential* texts and projects, capable of being adapted, but also some that might serve as a springboard for educators' own work. Students and contexts will vary, and we hope that the ideas presented here can provide examples of the vast opportunities that exist for using young adult literature to work toward social justice.

Teachers, counselors, and school leaders have the power and opportunity to guide, develop, encourage, and inspire the youth of today to be engaged, active citizens. We hope the texts, topics, and suggested projects in this book serve as a resource and support for all who are concerned with helping students to think critically and use their voices and actions to change their communities and the world for the better. It is our responsibility and our duty, as teachers, to engage our students with their worlds and to do so in thoughtful ways that recognize, address, and validate the humanity around them.

REFERENCES

Anderson, L. H. (1999). *Speak.* New York: Farrar Straus Giroux.
Bishop, R. S. (1990). Mirrors, windows, and sliding glass doors. *Perspectives: Choosing and using books for the classroom, 6*(3), ix–xi.
Bomer, R. & Bomer, K. (2001). *For a better world: Reading and writing for social action.* Portsmouth, NH: Heinemann.

Boyd, A. (2017). *Social justice literacies in the English classroom: Teaching practice in action*. New York: Teachers College Press.

Boyd, A. & Bereiter, T. (2017). "I don't really know what a fair portrayal is and what a stereotype is": Pluralizing transgender narratives with young adult literature. *English Journal, 107*(1), 13–18.

Boyd, A. & Dyches, J. (2017). Taking down walls: Countering dominant narratives of the immigrant experience through the teaching of *Enrique's Journey. The ALAN Review, 42*(2), 31–42.

Butcher, K. & Hinton, K. (2013). *Young adult literature: Exploration, evaluation, and appreciation* (3rd ed.). Boston, MA: Pearson.

Canadian Teachers' Federation & The Critical Thinking Consortium. (2010). *Social action projects: Making a difference K–4*. Ottawa, ON: Canadian Teachers Federation and The Critical Thinking Consortium.

Cart, M. (2010). *Young adult literature: From romance to realism*. Chicago, IL: American Library Association.

Cartledge, G., Gardner, R., & Ford, D. Y. (2009). *Diverse learners with exceptionalities: Culturally responsive teaching in the inclusive classroom*. Upper Saddle River, NJ: Pearson.

Clark, C. T. & Blackburn, M. V. (2009). Reading LGBT-themed literature with young people: What's possible? *English Journal, 98*(4), 25–32.

Cormier, R. (1974). *The chocolate war*. New York: Pantheon.

Crenshaw, K. (1989). Demarginalizing the intersection of race and sex: A Black feminist critique of antidiscrimination doctrine, feminist theory and antiracist politics. *Chicago Legal Forum: Feminism in the Law: Theory, Practice and Criticism*, 139–167.

Curry, A. (2001). Where is Judy Blume? Controversial fiction for older children and young adults. *Journal of Youth Services in Libraries, 14*(3), 24–33.

Darragh, J. J. (2015). Exploring the effects of reading young adult literature that portrays people with disabilities in the inclusion classroom. *Electronic Journal for Inclusive Education, 3*(4).

Darragh, J. J. & Radmer, E. (2016). Connecting to their lives: Young adult literature and student achievement. *Making Literacy Connections, 31*, 18–30.

Denzin, J. (2013). Boundaries for contemporary literature: The role of censorship and choice. *Journal of Adolescent & Adult Literacy, 57*(1), 7–11.

Downey, A. L. (2005). The transformative power of drama: Bringing literature and social justice to life. *English Journal, 95*(1), 33–39.

Epstein, S. E. (2013). Independent voices, social insight, and action: An analysis of a social action project. *Journal of Social Studies Research, 37*, 123–136.

Epstein, S. E. (2014). *Teaching civic literacy projects: Student engagement with social problems*. New York: Teachers College Press.

Freeman, E. & Lehman, B. A. (2001). *Global perspectives in children's literature*. Needham Heights, MA: Allyn & Bacon.

Gee, J. (2015). *Social linguistics and literacies: Ideology in discourses* (2nd ed.). New York: Routledge Falmer.

Glasgow, J. N. (2001). Teaching social justice through young adult literature. *English Journal, 90*(6), 54–61.

Glaus, M. (2014). Text complexity and young adult literature. *Journal of Adolescent & Adult Literacy, 57*(5), 407–416.

Gold, R. (2012). *Being Emily*. Tallahassee, FL: Bella Books.

Green, J. & Levithan, D. (2011). *Will Grayson, Will Grayson*. New York: Penguin.

Hayn, J. A., Kaplan, J. S., Nolen, A. L., & Olvey, H. A. (2015). *Young adult nonfiction: Gateway to the common core*. Lanham, MD: Rowman & Littlefield.

Hill, C. (Ed.). (2014). *Critical merits of young adult literature: Coming of age*. New York: Routledge.

Hinton, S. E. (1967). *The outsiders*. New York: Viking.

Ivey, G. & Johnston, P. H. (2013). Engagement with young adult literature: Outcomes and processes. *Reading Research Quarterly, 48*(3), 255–275.

Jones, J. B. (2011). *There you will find me*. Nashville, TN: Thomas Nelson.

Kurkjian, C. & Livingston, N. (2007). The importance of children's literature in a global society. *The Reading Teacher, 60*(6), 594–602.

Larrick, N. (1965). The all-white world of children's books. *The Saturday Review*, 63–65.

Miller, s. j. (2014). Text complexity and comparable literary merit in young adult literature. *The ALAN Review, 41*(2), 44–55.

Morrell, E. (2005). Critical English education. *English Education, 37*(4), 312–321.

Nazario, S. (2014). *Enrique's journey (The young adult adaptation): The true story of a boy determined to reunite with his mother.* New York: Random House.

Nilsen, A. P. & Donelson, K. L. (2012). *Literature for today's young adults* (9th ed.). Boston: Pearson.

Pascal, F. (1986). *Best friends.* Sweet Valley High twins and friends series. New York: Bantam Books.

Rosenblatt, L. M. (1933/1995). *Literature as exploration.* New York: The Modern Language Association of America.

Simmons, A. M. (2012). Class on fire: Using *The Hunger Games* trilogy to encourage social action. *Journal of Adolescent & Adult Literacy, 56*(1), 22–34.

Sokoll, T. (2013). Representations of trans youth in young adult literature: A report and a suggestion. *Young Adult Library Services,* 23–26.

Soter, A. O. (1999). *Young adult literature and the new literacy theories.* New York: Teachers College Press.

Stine, R. L. (1989). *The new girl.* Fear Street series. New York: Simon Pulse.

Toliver, S. R. (2018). Imagining new hopescapes: Expanding black girls' windows and mirrors. *Research on Diversity in Youth Literature, 1,* Article 3.

Trueman, T. (2000). *Stuck in neutral.* New York: HarperCollins.

We Need Diverse Books. (2018). Media kit. Retrieved from https://diversebooks.org/media-kit/.

1

BULLYING

Bullying, or "unwanted, aggressive behavior" ("Facts about Bullying," 2017), happens in many spaces—the workplace, the mall, and even the home. Reasons that are often given by perpetrators of bullying include a person's gender, sexual orientation, or appearance. Many times, however, bullying happens without an attempt to justify—only for the bully to assert their power over another individual.

There are myriad forms that bullying assumes. Verbal insults, such as name-calling, teasing, and threats are common manifestations of bullying, as well as physical actions, such as hitting, pushing, or harming a person's possessions. In more recent years, social bullying, such as spreading a rumor about someone, and cyberbullying, causing harm to a person through technological means such as social media, have become more widely identified. Hinduja and Patchin (2016) of the Cyberbullying Research Center found that 22.5 percent of students surveyed in their 5,707 nationally representative teen sample ages twelve to seventeen reported having been bullied through mean or hurtful comments online *in the previous thirty days* [emphasis added].

Female teens disclosed having experienced more cyberbullying over the course of their lifetimes. Yet the types of cyberbullying differed according to gender: "girls were more likely to say someone spread rumors about them online while boys were more likely to say that someone threatened to hurt them online" (Hinduja & Patachin, 2016, para. 5). With the prevalence of social media including Facebook, Instagram, Twitter, and Snapchat, cyberbullying has increasingly demanded attention in schools.

There is often confusion in defining what actually constitutes bullying, or even a backlash against labeling bullying at all, as some feel that the term is overly used. Consistent in definitions of bullying are concepts of power and repetition—that is, the perpetrator holds some form of physical, emotional, financial, or structural power over their victim, and the behavior occurs frequently and/or recurrently. In noting the difference between being rude or mean and being a bully, Whitson (2016) writes, "Rudeness is often unintentional, mean behavior very much aims to hurt or depreciate someone" (para. 15), but bullying denotes actions that are "intentionally hurtful to others" (para. 22) and, importantly, bullies "keep doing it, with no sense of regret or remorse—even when targets of bullying show or express their hurt or tell the aggressors to stop" (para. 23).

Being clear about what bullying is—and what it is not—helps to avoid an overuse of and therefore desensitization to the concept. Brown (2008) suggests that members of society take care to name the behavior explicitly, rather than lumping all incidents of harassment under the umbrella of bullying: "If it's sexual harassment, call it sexual harassment; if it's homophobia, call it homophobia" (para. 4). Among the list of positive effects of specifically naming behaviors, such an approach "helps us educate children about their rights, affirms their realities, encourages more complex and meaningful solutions, opens up a dialogue" (para. 4).

Furthermore, "Many youth perceive 'bullying' as a childish word and phenomenon . . . that happens in elementary school" (Hughes & Laffier, 2016, p. 8), while others are reluctant to admit that they have been bullied out of shame or fear (Peskin, Tortolero, & Markham, 2006). Thus, it is crucial, especially with young people, to provide information about what comprises bullying and to treat the topic with a serious and critical lens.

Addressing bullying with our youth is especially imperative because its damaging effects are far-reaching. Individuals have noted prolonged trauma from having been bullied in their youth. The Centers for Disease Control (2018) reported that being bullied "increases the risk for depression, anxiety, sleep difficulties, lower academic achievement, and dropping out of school" (Centers for Disease Control, 2018, p. 2). Bullying has also been linked to suicide and suicidal ideations (Kim & Leventhal, 2008). Both perpetrator and victim are worthy of consideration when discussing bullying. Although it is difficult to pinpoint one particular profile of a bully or victim, some patterns do exist for each, such as bullies' needs for social control or having experienced negative environments themselves, or victims' vulnerability and shyness.

The issue of bullying among youth also exhibits more structurally related patterns, as it appears often after the transition to middle school or in conjunction with environmental factors. Its pervasive, not isolated, nature illustrates that it is larger than one individual or case; it affects all of society. Thus, bullying is a complex issue that warrants educators' attention and action. It deserves consistent responsiveness in both our political conversations in terms of policies and protections as well as in schools with regard to recognizing, preventing, and confronting bullying among young people.

In this chapter, we focus on Meg Medina's (2013) *Yaqui Delgado Wants to Kick Your Ass* in order to emphasize the social problem of bullying with students. Although bullying can occur in many realms, we center specifically on bullying in a school context and with adolescent youth. We hope that through this text and topic, young people can understand the importance of being kind to one another and can recognize— and work to address—bullying that occurs in their environments. Because bullying has immediate and far-reaching effects, it is of extreme import that teachers work to ensure the safety of the youth in schools and classrooms.

YAQUI DELGADO WANTS TO KICK YOUR ASS

Yaqui Delgado Wants to Kick Your Ass begins with an eye-catching title and has a plot to match. The story follows a teenage female, Piedad (Piddy) Sanchez, who is bullied by another female, Yaqui Delgado, at her new school. Piddy struggles throughout to understand why her bully has targeted her and how she can avoid further strife, going to great lengths to conceal what is happening to her from her mother and school officials.

Cummins (2014) explains, "Possible motives for Yaqui's behavior include resentment that Yaqui's boyfriend admires Piddy's appearance and a wish to retain social dominance. Yaqui may think Piddy considers herself superior" (p. 4). The reasons are never made entirely clear, and readers learn very little about Yaqui except that she lives in a neighborhood that is a "rough beat" and in which, for example, police "found a kid shot through the head in the lobby of his building" (Medina, 2013, p. 130).

Having transferred from another high school to the one Yaqui attends, Piddy's position as a newcomer results in her precarious position. Physically assaulted by Yaqui and her posse on multiple occasions, including a vicious beating outside of her home, Piddy nonetheless evades exposing her offenders as long as possible. Her self-esteem, achievement in school, and relationship with her mother spiral downward as she struggles to deal with the situation and to make sense of the fact that bullying can happen at a school that supposedly has a zero-tolerance policy.

Piddy's experience is not the only instance of bullying within the novel. Her classmate Rob is the target of homophobic harassment, and Piddy's former neighbor, Joey Halper, lives with an abusive father whose physical assaults ultimately leave his mother hospitalized. Although a different form of destructive behavior, the Halpers' story is integral to Piddy's, as this narrative runs parallel to her recognizing her own abuse and her willingness to seek help. Finally, Piddy does disclose her bully to school administrators, and with the help of video evidence is able to explain and validate what has happened to her. In a realistic ending, however, Yaqui is not removed from the school, but rather Piddy transfers back to her previous institution. Although Piddy is removed from further physical harm, she continues to deal with the long-term effects of her distress.

We chose *Yaqui Delgado Wants to Kick Your Ass* because the book illustrates the intricacies and consequences of bullying through an emotionally captivating story and narrative tone. The story of Piddy illustrates the downward spiral that verbal and physical harassment can cause while simultaneously affirming the resilience and strength of a person who is bullied—both of which are important lessons for young readers.

TEACHING STRATEGIES

Before Reading

Students will have likely heard the words *bully* and *bullying* in their elementary school contexts. While counselors and teachers educate young people about bullying, with older students these notions can be complicated by discussing the implications of power they contain and their ramifications. Teachers can therefore begin by asking students what they already know about bullying and by creating a web on the board from students' descriptions. Then, students can go online and research common definitions of bullying and record those as well. In small groups, they can create a one-sentence definition of bullying that captures their research and class brainstorming. This will establish a baseline to revisit as they read the novel and possibly revise as they see Yaqui's behavior and how it affects Piddy.

As part of this discussion and research, teachers can ask students to consider questions including: *Why do people bully? What reasons do bullies give for their behavior, if they do? Who are some famous bullies and what did they do?* This will help students further pinpoint what constitutes bullying and have examples to draw upon in classroom discourse. As noted in the previous section, an important aspect to consider as teachers lead students through this conversation is the difference between "being mean" and "being a bully."

Teachers might provide students with scenarios to consider from popular media, current events, or historic examples, and even ask students to design their own for their peers to identify. For example, students might consider the famous Biff in the movie *Back to the Future*, O'Doyle in *Billy Madison*, or Regina George in *Mean Girls*, and discuss if these are instances of bullying and how. Older students might even read Whitson's (2016) article that distinguishes bullying from being mean.

Discussions about why people bully might lead to controversy; thus, teachers should equip themselves with strategies to talk about issues of *difference* as they arise, including disabilities, sexual orientations, and the gender spectrum, for instance, and how these may lead to fear and consequently intimidation, harassment, or mistreatment. They might refer to instances from history, looking at, for example, the bullying that occurred during school integration in the South with the Little Rock Nine, the African American students who attended a previously all-white school in 1957. They could view a video overview (CBS, 2017) and name the forms of bullying they identify and the basis of this harassment. It will be important for teachers to remind students, however, that hate crimes are different from bullying, as are protests. In the instances in the video, the focus on repeated aggressive behavior constitutes bullying.

Students could also view scenes from the documentary *Bully* (Foudy, Hirsch, Lowen, & Waitt, 2011). This film was created in the wake of the death of Tyler Long, an adolescent male who was bullied so intensely that he died by suicide. Following several students over the course of one school year, the documentary illustrates various scenarios in which youth are bullied. One student has been diagnosed with Asperger's Syndrome, another has come out as lesbian, and another is small in physical size. These poignant stories portray not only the effects of bullying on the victim but on their families as well.

Showing both large-scale examples of bullying such as those that required government intervention in the Civil Rights Movement as well as smaller-scale individual instances can help students consider the notions of power involved and the many factors that affect bullying. After watching, they could chart the consequences of bullying and who it impacts to visually illustrate its far-reaching ramifications.

Once students locate and view examples of bullying, teachers can then ask them to return to one of the scenes or instances they studied and to disrupt it. As a spectator, they could design a way that the bullying could be interrupted and addressed by a bystander, the perpetrator, or the victim. Helping students imagine how to act in such situations through tangible means can empower them. Pinpointing times and places where bullying can be stopped or prevented illustrates that bullying behavior is not inevitable. This activity can also be the basis for during and after reading activities in which students apply the concept of disruption to the novel.

During Reading

Given this foundation, as students read the novel, teachers can ask them at various points what could have been done differently to address the situation with Yaqui and Piddy as it unfolds. For instance, teachers can ask students to recreate scenes, prompting them with inquiries such as: *What could have been done when Yaqui throws the milk across the cafeteria? What could have been done during or after Yaqui attacks Piddy outside of her home? When else might someone at school have intervened, and how?*

This should not, however, be conducted in a way that simplifies the issue; it is clear that Piddy has valid reasons for not wanting to report

Yaqui. She describes how when she reflects on the milk incident, it weighs on her "with shame" (p. 50), knowing that she must be perceived as weak. She later tells Lila after the physical assault that if she tells her mother and it becomes an issue at school, "Yaqui will just get me worse next time—her or one of her friends" (p. 165). Her fear is thus real and warranted and should be treated as such.

Teachers can therefore ask students to deeply consider the possible ramifications of disruptions to bullying, considering, for example, in their proposed actions questions such as: *Who might be hurt in the process? What would happen to Piddy if your solution occurred? Which seems better—to stay quiet in this scene or to act?* Exploring these possibilities further illustrates the complexity of bullying.

Students might also make a list of possible reasons (those given in the text and not) why Yaqui might be bullying Piddy. Yaqui says it is related to her boyfriend Alfredo, and yet Piddy has had no interaction with him, except perhaps when he and another male catcall her in the school yard. Piddy also learns that the way she walks may have attracted attention, which makes her question her own body. Students might speculate that Yaqui's home life is not positive, given that readers are told by a character in the novel who is a police officer that she lives in a neighborhood plagued by crime. Furthermore, Yaqui's need to assert power is worthy of discussion.

Teachers might ask: *What is Yaqui trying to prove? Why might Yaqui need to claim her dominance over Piddy? Why might Yaqui's friends go along with her attacks?* They could imagine and write scenes that answer these questions since such little is known about these areas in the book and often in portrayals of bullies.

While the situation with Piddy and Yaqui has ambiguous root causes, the instance in which a perpetrator writes "Homo" on Piddy's peer's locker contains clear motivations. Teachers can address this instance of bullying as well and whether or not Piddy did the right thing—careful not to question whether or she should have advocated for Rob (because such a question would imply it is OK to bully for reasons related to sexual orientation)—but inquiring if marking out the negative words was the appropriate solution or if this instance of bullying could have been disrupted differently as well. With a partner, students could brainstorm alternative action plans for Piddy.

Teachers can also ask students to read critically the school's response to the situation with Piddy's and Rob's locker, noting the author's commentary on the contradiction of the school's "Bully-Free Zone" posters juxtaposed with punishing Yaqui for attempting to help her friend. Teachers can ask: *What are the bullying policies at our school? Do you think the administrator's treatment of Yaqui was fair? Why or why not? How else might the school have dealt with the situation with Yaqui and Rob?*

A school administrator might serve as a guest speaker in the classroom to explain to students the school policy and to answer questions. The teacher can then ask student groups to revisit their definitions of bullying and apply them to both Piddy's and Rob's situations, discerning if the instances fit their definitions and/or if they want to revise their definitions based on these examples. Groups can present how their definitions are reflected in each situation.

Contemplating what is right or wrong can lead to a discussion of Piddy's mother, Clara, who is an important character in the story and reflects a hard-working single mother who wants the best for her daughter. Clara has particular ideas about how females should act and dress. Piddy's mother's personality may be part of the reason Piddy is afraid to tell her about the bullying at school, while Lila, her mother's best friend, is ultimately the adult that Piddy confides in about her torture.

Readers might conduct character analyses through drawing each figure and might even compare the two women through Piddy's eyes. Teachers can ask: *When should or could have Piddy told her mother? Did Lila make the right decision in keeping Piddy's assault a secret and aiding her in concealment at other moments? What do youth want in an adult when they confide about instances such as bullying?*

Cyberbullying, a form of harassment in which social media or other online sources are used to badger an individual, occurs in the novel when the video of Yaqui assaulting Piddy is placed online. Piddy is humiliated not only by the incident itself but also by its existence in cyberspace for all to witness. The video has over seven hundred views by the time Darlene shares it with Piddy, whose response is "I'm ruined" (p. 172). Yet the video is what solidifies evidence of Yaqui's behavior when she tries to deny it and what prompts adult intervention.

Teachers can ask students to speculate how bullying is different in today's era as opposed to, for example, their parents' and grandparents' times in school. Lila tells Piddy, "There's always a Yaqui in every school, in every place in the world," but Piddy avows "it's different now" (p. 219). Readers can discuss: *Why might it be easier to bully someone online than in person? What are the possible consequences for cyberbullying for all involved? How does online bullying occur, besides just this example? What can be done to stop it?*

As the novel unfolds, students can keep a list of the effects or consequences that Yaqui's bullying has on Piddy, and they can compare these to their previous research and the documentary they viewed. Piddy stays home from school feigning sickness, skips school altogether, radically changes, thinking "Piddy's dead" (p. 168), and no longer acts like herself, wanting to leave school. Even after she transfers schools at the end of the novel, she remains afraid. Her guidance counselor tells her "trauma takes a while to work through" (p. 256), thus exemplifying that the ramifications of bullying do not end when the bully is removed.

While creating the list of reasons for Yaqui's bullying will explore her character in depth and perhaps showhow she is different from Piddy, also worth noting are the potential similarities between Yaqui and Piddy. Piddy frequently mentions the fact that both adolescent females are Latina, noting, "Yaqui and me, we should be two *hermanas*, a sisterhood of Latinas. We eat the same food. We talk the same way . . . but instead, we're worlds apart" (p. 56).

Students might create visual renderings of each character, noting their similarities and differences. They could complete a character sketch, which teachers might find from a number of templates (e.g., White, 2014). This will help illustrate how not all members of one cultural group are the same and yet they may have some overlapping aspects. And although Piddy feels a certain camaraderie with Yaqui around their cultural affiliations, despite this potential "in group" status, the situation persists.

As part of this reflection on Latinx culture, teachers can also play the numerous songs that Piddy mentions as they arise in the novel. They might ask students how these references help set the scene and enrich the vicarious experience of the reader. Readers learn that Piddy's mother was an astute piano player, having studied for years in Cuba, but she stopped after she moved to the United States and was later abandoned by Piddy's father. She encourages Piddy to listen to Bach instead of her culture's music.

Teachers might play students an example of the *tumbao* (p. 51), which Piddy's mother supposedly played well (e.g., Goldcoco, 2017). They could then compare this to a piece by Bach (e.g., Halidon Music, 2017) and ask students to identify the differences between the two pieces. They could then consider what this shows about Piddy's mother—both in terms of her own personal transformation as well as her attitude toward Latin culture.

Students might also enjoy hearing Paquita la del Barrio's "Rata de Dos Patas" and reading the lyrics (e.g., Canalestrellatv, 2013), which incites the women at Lila's Avon party to sing along loudly and about which Piddy states, "It's a hit in Spanish, but I have to wonder how it would do in English" (p. 110). Students can consider why the women love this song and if Piddy's speculation is correct. They might also brainstorm songs in English that might not translate well to another cultural context, recognizing that Piddy's point is reciprocal.

Students can also keep a running dictionary of Spanish words as they arise in the novel. Piddy; her mother, Clara; and Lila often draw upon Spanish phrases to express themselves and their opinions clearly. For instance, when Clara sees Yaqui on their walk from the grocery store, she tells her "'no one decent hangs out in a school yard. . . . Look at that one. . . . A savage on the street. *Qué chusma'*" (p. 54) and then she goes onto to say "*Son unas cualquieras*" (p. 55). Her language is reflective of "her worst nightmare of what a Latin girl can become in the United States" (pp. 55–56).

If there are Spanish speakers in the room who want to help define these phrases, teachers could draw on their expertise, or students could look up the words Clara uses and determine what message she is trying to convey to Piddy. Students might relate these also to lessons their own guardians teach them. Teachers can ask: *What does the Spanish language add to the novel? Why would the author include these expressions and words as she does?*

After Reading

The ending of the novel is, in many ways, anticlimactic. Yaqui is not punished or kicked out of school for her behavior. Adolescents, many expecting happy endings and believing in justice, may be highly disappointed and frustrated by the final scenes. Lila even says, "The wrong person is paying the price for this mess. . . . The wrong person is getting kicked out" (p. 254). Teachers can ask students if this is true and if justice was served—or if that even matters here. Students can organize and engage in a structured debate surrounding this issue.

They can then be challenged to write their own alternative endings, including what might happen to Joey, Yaqui's love interest. They may envision that Piddy runs away with him or meets him later in life, or they may imagine a scene in which Yaqui is punished for her behavior. They will also likely have questions about Piddy's "safety transfer," so teachers should familiarize themselves with local policies or aid students in acquiring if such is a possibility in their own school district. Again, a guest speaker might be helpful to inform students and answer their questions.

And yet, while Piddy is the victim of bullying, her story is also one of empowerment and hope, and this should not be overlooked. Students can watch the author Meg Medina's speech at the National Book Festival (Library of Congress, 2014), in which she shares that she did not want to write a story about bullying but about Piddy and how she gets herself out of the hole she finds herself in—how her culture, her family, and her sense of self were the things that carried her through trying times. Students can view this video and reflect on instances in the book where Piddy shows strength. Adolescent readers might also be enthused to get to know the author's autobiographical reasons for writing the novel. Watching the video could also lead students to tweet or simply email Meg Medina with their reactions.

Purportedly on IMDb (2018), development for a television show based on the novel *Yaqui Delgado Wants to Kick Your Ass* is underway. Students might therefore be excited to create their own cast of characters and even scene additions or rewrites for the screen version. They might explore what famous actors and actresses would serve best in the roles and why, using the text as evidence to demonstrate their understandings of personalities and appearances. They might even make digital trailers ("Book Trailers," n.d.) and include music from the text, referencing the songs mentioned above that are included in scenes from the book.

In order to fully analyze the issue of bullying, students can further unpack the storyline of Mr. Halper, whose abuse of his wife is mentioned throughout the novel and culminates at the end when she is hospitalized. Teachers can ask students: *Does bullying only happen among children and adolescents? In what ways is Mr. Halper a bully, and in what ways is he not? How does this storyline apply to Piddy—what does it make her realize about herself? Why would Medina include this as a subplot? How does it drive the narrative?* Discussing domestic abuse in the classroom is a sensitive topic and thus teacher's discretion is encouraged. Perhaps a school counselor or trained community member could be present to assist students in working through this difficult topic.

Finally, in reference to the end of the novel, students can expand their research on policies related to bullying at their own school to their state and across the nation. Teachers can provide guided research questions or data collection tables so that students' work is pointed toward examining various prevention programs and punishments, looking specifically at what offenses the school regulates and how. Gathering this data will help them more readily conduct social action.

IDEAS FOR SOCIAL ACTION

While the ending of the novel is realistic, and this should be honored, asking students to address and work to remedy bullying in ways that are more direct is warranted when teaching the book. Borrowing from the national survey on bullying (Hinduja & Patchin, 2016), students might create a school-based survey, taken anonymously, to collect data on bullying in their own school. They could disaggregate results to report the different forms most prevalent in their school (e.g., cyberbullying) and how they may be different according to grade level and gender. Once these statistics are mined, students can share these with administrators and include targeted suggestions for addressing their findings.

Students can complement this work by using their research on their school and nationwide policies on bullying to compose additional recommendations for their administrators and other stakeholders. Once data has been collected on district, state, and national policies, they can determine what components seem most appropriate and helpful while eliminating those that are unrealistic or obstructive. They might suggest or create an anonymous reporting system if one does not exist, like the one that Rob used to help Piddy. They might also designate one trustworthy adult in the school to whom students can go if they are being bullied or know someone who is. Finally, they could call for the institution of prevention programs, or they might create their own awareness campaigns based on their researched definitions of bullying or through signs for recognizing bullying and ways to address it.

Students can also create a presentation for their peers from this extensive local and broad research on bullying and its long-term consequences and share it with the entire school. They might also design and implement appropriate presentations for elementary school students, serving as models to younger students for what to do if harassment occurs. In order to solicit student empathy and understanding, they might use narratives of bullying, especially from the perspectives of victims, from books or popular media. They could invite students at their school to share their own stories (anonymously) if they choose—perhaps having a special issue of a school newspaper or newsletter on bullying.

From a perhaps more affirming stance, students might also determine ways to celebrate difference and emphasize that ability, sexual orientation, social class, and the gender spectrum make individuals unique rather than provide grounds for mistreatment. They could create public service announcements that air during school news broadcasts or visual materials to be displayed throughout the school in hallways, classrooms, and the cafeteria that promote positive messages about inclusivity. They could further brainstorm and implement ways to applaud, rather than denigrate, others. Such preventative measures, rather than only reactive sentences, are necessary if teachers, parents, and other stakeholders truly wish to get at the heart of bullying.

SUPPLEMENTAL RESOURCES

Canonical Companions

Of Mice and Men by John Steinbeck
Antigone by Sophocles
Jane Eyre by Charlotte Brontë
Lord of the Flies by William Golding

Connected Young Adult Literature

13 Reasons Why by Jay Asher
The Chocolate War by Robert Cormier

Burn by Suzanne Phillips

Connected Music

"Rata de Dos Patos" by Paquita la del Barrio
"Fugue in D Minor" by Bach
Tumbao on piano

REFERENCES

"Book Trailers." (n.d.). Retrieved from https://creativeeducator.tech4learning.com/v07/lessons/ Entice_Your_Reader.

Brown, L. M. (2008). 10 ways to move beyond bully prevention (and why we should). *Education Week.* Retrieved from https://www.edweek.org/ew/articles/2008/03/05/26brown.h27. html.

Canalestrellatv. (2013, January 7). *Paquita la del barria canta "rata de dos patas"* [Video file]. Retrieved from https://www.youtube.com/watch?v=K5A-QyriVl4.

CBS Evening News. (2017, September 25). *Eight of the surviving "Little Rock Nine" students recall milestone* [Video file]. Retrieved from https://www.youtube.com/watch?v=7Hc-9ZWe6wk.

Centers for Disease Control. (2018). Preventing bullying. Retrieved from https://www.cdc.gov/ violenceprevention/pdf/bullying-factsheet508.pdf.

Cummins, A. (2014). Using young adult literature to provide case studies for discussion of bullying: An analysis of the 2014 Pura Belpré award winner. *Texas Journal of Literacy Education, 2*(1), 2–12.

"Effects of Bullying." (2015). Retrieved from http://www.pacer.org/bullying/resources/stats. asp.

"Facts about Bullying." (2017, September 28). Retrieved from https://www.stopbullying.gov/ media/facts/index.html.

Foudy, S., Hirsch, L., Lowen, C., & Waitt, C. (Producers), & Hirsch, L. (Director). (2011). *Bully* [Documentary]. United States: The Weinstein Company.

Goldcoco (2017, July 14). *Salsa piano tumbao 2* [Video file]. Retrieved from https://www. youtube.com/watch?v=qqeOnrqbYLA.

Halidon Music. (2017, March 21). *Bach piano solo* [Video file]. Retrieved from https://www. youtube.com/watch?v=cOrKeFUZSJ0.

Hinduja, S. & Patchin, J. W. (2016). 2016 cyberbullying data. Retrieved from https:// cyberbullying.org/2016-cyberbullying-data.

Hughes, J. & Laffier, J. L. (2016). Portrayals of bullying in young adult literature: Considerations for schools. *Canadian Journal of Education, 39*(3), 1–24.

IMDb. (2018). *Yaqui Delgado wants to kick your ass* [Television series]. Retrieved from https:/ /www.imdb.com/title/tt6856430/.

Kim, Y. S. & Leventhal, B. (2008). Bullying and suicide: A review. *International Journal of Adolescent Mental Health, 20*(2), 133–154.

Library of Congress. (2014, November 14). Meg Medina: 2014 National Book Festival [Video file]. Retrieved from https://www.youtube.com/watch?v=7Hc-9ZWe6wk.

Medina, M. (2013). *Yaqui Delgado wants to kick your ass.* Somerville, MA: Candlewick Press.

Peskin, M. F., Tortolero, S. R., & Markham, C. M. (2006). Bullying and victimization among black and Hispanic adolescents. *Adolescence, 41*(163), 467–484.

White, R. (2014). Character sketch template. Retrieved from http://fictionfoundry.alumni. columbia.edu/character_sketch_template.

Whitson, S. (2016, September 7). Rude vs. mean vs. bullying: Defining the differences. *Huff-post*. Retrieved from https://www.huffpost.com/entry/bullying_b_2188819.

2

GLOBAL POVERTY

In 1948, the United Nations adopted the Universal Declaration of Human Rights (UDHR). Together with the International Covenant on Civil and Political Rights and the International Covenant on Economic, Social and Cultural Rights, these three documents comprise the International Bill of Human Rights (United Nations, n.d.), rights that all human beings should have access to, regardless of country of origin, race, ethnicity, gender, ability, or socioeconomic status.

There are two articles within the International Bill of Rights that are particularly relevant to children under the age of eighteen. Article 25 states:

> Everyone has the right to a standard of living adequate for the health and well-being of himself and of his family, including food, clothing, housing and medical care and necessary social services, and the right to security in the event of unemployment, sickness, disability, widowhood, old age or other lack of livelihood in circumstances beyond his control. (United Nations, 2003, p. 5)

Likewise, Article 26 declares, "Everyone has the right to education. Education shall be free, at least in the elementary and fundamental stages. Elementary education shall be compulsory. Technical and professional education shall be made generally available and higher education shall be equally accessible to all on the basis of merit" (United Nations, 2003, p. 5).

However, despite this Declaration, many people living in developing countries with extreme poverty do not have access to these and other basic human rights. According to the United Nations, 783 million people, almost 10 percent of the world, lived below the international poverty line ($1.90 per day) in 2016. These same people often don't have access to clean drinking water (Poverty Resolutions, 2018), education, or health care. In fact, every day over twenty-one thousand children die due to poverty-related impacts (Poverty Resolutions, 2018).

In 2017, there were twenty-eight countries where people lived on less than $1,000 per year (Martin, 2018). Topping that list are South Sudan ($246/year), Burundi ($339/year), and Malawi ($342/year) (Martin, 2018). The regions with the greatest number of people living below the poverty line are Southern Asia and sub-Saharan Africa; nearly 70 percent of people living in extreme poverty come from countries in those regions (United Nations, n.d.).

Young adults often do not know a great deal about other countries and the lives of people around the world. Western news and media tend to focus on events that take place in North America, and, as such, it is easy to be unaware of the plight of others across the globe. In this chapter we focus on the issue of global poverty. Because as human beings we should care for the welfare of, and support the access to, basic human rights for all people, we suggest a unit of study that thoughtfully incorporates international perspectives, focusing on those developing nations that suffer from extreme poverty, food instability, and a general lack of resources.

I WILL ALWAYS WRITE BACK

I Will Always Write Back by Caitlin Alifirenka and Martin Ganda (2015) shares the true story of pen pals Caitlin from Pennsylvania and Martin from Zimbabwe. What started as an assignment for seventh-grade English class turned into a lifelong friendship between the two, and as the story progresses, readers experience both sides of the friendship as it deepens and grows.

Over the years, through his letters, Martin begins to open up to Caitlin about his family, schooling, and the financial troubles that jeopardize his completing his education. Simultaneously, Caitlin is leading a typical North American teenage life, while also learning more about other cultures, developing countries, and Martin's needs, as well as the barriers he is facing in making his dreams come true.

For over six years Caitlin and Martin wrote to each other, developing their friendship and supporting each other in very different ways. The epilogue of the book shares what the pen pals are doing now and why they decided to share with the world, through this book, their unlikely friendship that changed both of their lives for the better.

In this chapter, we use the text *I Will Always Write Back* to address global poverty because it provides an individual, relatable look at the topic. Additionally, unlike some of the other focal YA texts in this book, *I Will Always Write Back* is especially suitable for students in middle school, as it begins when Caitlin is in seventh grade and does not depict mature language or themes that might be inappropriate for a younger audience.

This text not only depicts the challenges poverty can present to young adults around the world but also shows the power of writing and friendship in a way that might inspire students to learn about different cultures, and in doing so, learn more about themselves and the power they possess to positively impact the lives of others.

TEACHING STRATEGIES

Before Reading

There are a variety of websites that offer information regarding extreme poverty around the world. The World Bank's Poverty and Equity Data Portal provides current data "on poverty, inequality, and shared prosperity. The portal allows you to explore several poverty and inequality indicators for countries and regions as well as explore countries by various income levels" (World Bank, 2018, para. 1).

Similarly, students can peruse the "Global Extreme Poverty" section of the "Our World in Data" website that offers historical perspectives, current data, future projections, and colorful charts and graphs in conjunction with the data presented (Roser & Ortiz-Ospina, 2017) in order to have a better understanding of poverty in developing countries.

Students can also investigate the United Nations 17 Sustainable Development Goals: a call for action by all countries—poor, rich and middle-income—to promote prosperity while protecting the planet. They recognize that ending poverty must go hand-in-hand with strategies that build economic growth and addresses a range of social needs including education, health, social protection, and job opportunities, while tackling climate change and environmental protection. (United Nations, n.d., para. 1)

For each goal, facts and figures, general information, links, and suggestions regarding "What can I do about it?" are provided. Teachers can put students into groups and have them explore these various websites, then use a jigsaw approach to share and consolidate information they have gained. Then students can, for example, create a visual of the information they feel is most important or information specific to Zimbabwe, the homeland of Martin in the book *I Will Always Write Back*, and refer back to their visual creation while reading the text.

The Teaching Tolerance website (1991–2018) offers lesson plans geared toward introducing students to the complexity of global poverty. For example, the lesson plan "Education Evaluation" begins with an analysis of the International Declaration of Human Rights mentioned above, suggesting that teachers "explain to students that according to the Declaration of Human Rights, 'Every person is entitled to certain rights—simply by the fact that they are a human being'" (para. 3).

The lesson plan continues with students evaluating how well the world is doing when it comes to providing a free, equal, quality education to youth, discussing the long-term implications of children not having access to education, and brainstorming what can be done about this issue.

The *New York Times* shares a promising lesson plan that guides students in learning "about some of the ways the developing world is vulnerable to the impact and effects of natural disasters. They then investigate some 'natural disaster hotspots' around the globe and assess how vulnerable these areas are" (Hambouz & Eisenhauer, 2006, para. 1). Teachers might follow up with this lesson plan by having students search current news sources to track various natural disasters that might be occurring, as well as the relief efforts and impacts such disasters create. (See also chapter 12, Environmental Protection and Ecojustice, for further examples and ideas.)

There are a variety of documentaries that can help students to visualize specific developing countries as well as begin to understand the complexity of severe poverty on a global scale. For example, *The End of Poverty?* (Cobb, Leblanc, & Diaz, 2009) shares examples from Brazil, Venezuela, Bolivia, and Kenya, among others, while providing facts and statistics regarding the prevalence of global poverty, such as "24,000 people die every day from hunger and hunger-related diseases"; "Less than 5% of the world's population live in the United States. We are consuming over 25% of the world's resources and creating roughly 30% of its major pollution"; "Almost one third of the world's population has no access to affordable clean water"; and "The richest 1% of the world's population owns 32% of the wealth."

Teachers can pose these statistics as questions to the students before viewing the film in order to determine what they already know about economic inequalities around the world. The film focuses on the history of colonization dating back five hundred years as well as the systemic structures that are in place that keep developing nations from advancing economically. Teachers can lead students in revisiting these statements after they view the film and lead discussion regarding inequalities in the world today, how the world got here, and what, potentially, can be done in the future.

The Netflix docuseries *Daughters of Destiny* (Mussman & Roth, 2017) follows five girls from some of the poorest communities in India. Children from these "slums" are selected to attend a boarding school, Shanti Bhavan, where they are fed and educated, expected to go on to college and graduate, then go forth to serve and support others in their communities. With five different episodes following the students of Shanti Bhavan over many years, this collection can be shown in segments throughout a unit of study on global poverty.

In conjunction with the series, teachers can lead students in discussing questions like *How does access to education help the girls? What challenges does being one of the chosen to attend the school present to the students? What are your thoughts on this type of school/system for combatting extreme poverty? Is it/will it be/can it be successful? Why or why not?* After reading *I Will Always Write Back*, students can discuss whether a school like Shanti Bhavan would have been successful in Martin's town and brainstorm what parts of such a system can transcend cultures and what parts are location specific.

Of all the documentaries available, *Poverty, Inc.* (Mauren & Miller, 2016) may have the most promise for classroom use as it shares the (perhaps unintended) effects of powerful developed nations donating goods to people in developing countries. *Poverty, Inc.* demonstrates the impacts of tariffs and import duties on developing countries as well as how devastation from natural disasters is exacerbated when communities are not structurally sound. When disasters do happen, kind-hearted people often step in to help. However, this help can lead to unintended negative consequences.

One specific example that students can analyze is the aftereffects of the 2010 earthquake in Haiti. *Poverty, Inc.* explains, "It makes us feel good to help . . . and then we don't let go. . . . They claim that in Haiti alone there are 10,000 NGOs. . . . They keep trying to find ways to give away free stuff . . . as if they don't want the Haitians to stand up for themselves."

Using a specific example of a man who started his own business creating and selling solar panels in Haiti and was successfully able to employ many Haitians who needed jobs—until people from the United States donated solar panels to the country and drove him out of business—teachers can help students in identifying and debating the pros and cons of nongovernmental organizations (NGOs) and the "industry of charity."

Teachers can also use information from this documentary to inspire media analysis. For example, the documentary explains, "The media keeps telling Africans that Africa is poor. . . . Africa has always been a reservoir for resources for the rest of the world. . . . The people here are not stupid. They are just disconnected from global trade." Teachers can facilitate analysis of this quote by asking questions like *In what ways does the media promote the "poorness" of Africa?*

To illustrate their point, *Poverty, Inc.* mentions the song "Do They Know It's Christmas?" by Band Aid 30. Created as a means by which to help people suffering from famine in Ethiopia, an analysis of this song can help students begin to unpack the complexity of extreme poverty in developing countries. In conjunction with a media analysis, students can analyze the lyrics to this specific song, whether they have watched the documentary or not.

As it is a bit dated, students might need to research the groups Band Aid, Band Aid 20, and Band Aid 30 (and the different iterations/re-

recordings of this song: 1984, 1989, 2004, 2014). They might seek to answer questions like *What musicians are part of these groups? What is their purpose? What was the inspiration for the first song and the re-recordings?*

After students have identified the good intentions of this group, they can begin an analysis of the lyrics of the song, identifying what messages the song is sending about the people of West Africa specifically, as well as the musicians' lived experiences in comparison to the people about whom they are singing.

In analyzing the lyrics, teachers can lead students in considering questions like *When bad things happen, do we forget what time of year it is? In what ways does highlighting the negative experiences a group is facing provide happiness and tranquility, as the song suggests? What do the members of Band Aid 30 have to gain by recording this song? How does this recording positively impact the lives of those whose story is being told (exploited)? What are some alternatives to having musicians from the United Kingdom and the United States sing this song that might have similar results?*

To identify positive examples of support for people in extreme poverty, students can look at the article "45 Organizations That Battle Poverty" (Raptim, 2018) and research the various organizations identified to learn about what they do. Using those as a guide, students can identify the qualities and practices they would like to see in an NGO with regard to helping people from developing countries become autonomous. They can create a checklist by which to analyze NGOs that have a mission of supporting those in extreme poverty and create a visual of their findings.

During Reading

I Will Always Write Back offers rich opportunities for researching a developing country of each student's choice. Specifically, students can research how childhood and schooling compares to that in North America, especially when families have limited resources. For example, Martin explains about his mother:

> My mother grew up in a rural village. . . . She was very clever and always was first in her class. The problem was that her family was dirt poor. They had no electricity and bathed in the rivers. My mother

stayed in school until fifth grade, but then her family could no longer afford to send her. She dropped out, and soon after, they sent her to work for my father's family because they could no longer afford to feed her, either . . . it was also common to send children to work for other families—one fewer mouth to feed. My mother worked in exchange for her food and keep, which still happens today. (p. 18)

Students can refer back to the International Bill of Rights and determine what, if any, of Martin's mother's basic human rights were not met as a child and what the repercussions of that may have been. Similarly, as they are reading, students can determine if Martin's educational rights, as described in the book, were being met or not, providing textual evidence to support their claims. They can brainstorm what would have to change in order for Martin's and his mother's rights to have been met, as well as what steps would have to be taken to do so.

In describing his own life in Chisamba Singles, "one of the worst slums, not only in Mutare but also in all of Zimbabwe" (p. 103), Martin explains:

Food shortages had become a real problem fights broke out daily, haggling over prices, or bartering gone bad. This was becoming common. As was domestic violence—I had always heard men beat their wives, since we lived in such close quarters, but not I would see it out in the streets as well. Nothing was being hidden anymore. AIDS, too, had become rampant. (p. 102)

Teachers can help students to consider: *What do you think is the connection between domestic violence and poverty? Disease and poverty? Is this also true for people in developed countries? Why or why not? What can be done to prevent domestic violence and chronic illness epidemics in locations with extreme poverty?*

As the book progresses, Caitlin learns more and more about African geography and follows the current events in various African countries. Students can identify the countries mentioned in the book (e.g., Mozambique, Zambia, Tanzania, Zimbabwe) on a map and learn more about their geographies as well as their culture, history, and current events.

To continue, they might investigate diseases that stem from lack of access to basic health care, clean water, and other resources, like cholera and malaria, which Martin describes in letters to Caitlin. Students can create a timeline to go with the map, tracking not only Martin's experiences as depicted in the book but also historical and political events in Zimbabwe that led it to having the economic struggles it has today.

Teachers can also guide students in creating a Venn diagram analyzing the lives of Caitlin and Martin. In some ways they are very similar (e.g., they both like music, go to school, etc.), but in other ways their lives are so different (e.g., Caitlin's family has multiple cars, she gets a job, etc.). Students can discuss *How were Caitlin and Martin able to become best friends despite all of their differences? How did they connect with one another? How can we all use our similarities to overcome differences in lifestyles, worldviews, and cultures?*

I Will Always Write Back mentions various musical artists throughout. For example, Martin describes his father singing as he returned home from work and that his father "loved the Rolling Stones, Cream, and Led Zeppelin too" (p. 22). Students can look at the lyrics and listen to the music of various songs by the aforementioned artists, and, using what they know about Martin's father, identify which songs in general and specific lyrics in particular they feel most closely relate to Martin's father.

Similarly, at times both Martin and Caitlin reference artists and lyrics of certain pop songs in their letters. For example, Caitlin sends Martin P!nk's "Most Girls," Baha Men's "Who Let the Dogs Out," and Eminem's "The Real Slim Shady." Martin mentions "friendship never ends" from the Spice Girls' song "Wannabe" and, "you are really larger than life as Backstreet said" (p. 163), referencing the Backstreet Boys' song of the same name. As these songs are a bit dated, students might identify current songs/lyrics that they could substitute for the ones mentioned in the text, providing explanations for their choices that demonstrate their understanding of both Martin and Caitlin.

Students might also listen to the songs/artists Martin references (Ricky Martin, Spice Girls, Backstreet Boys) and compare the mood and tone of these songs compared to those Martin's father enjoys. Teachers can have students consider: *What do you think Martin, a struggling boy from Zimbabwe, likes about these songs? In analyzing the mood, tone, instrumentation, and lyrics of the songs, what do you think Martin connects with/ enjoys the most and why? Based on these songs, what current songs/ artists do you think Martin would enjoy?*

In conjunction with this activity, in the book Martin refers to one Zimbabwean musician, Thomas Mapfumo. Students can listen to some Mapfumo songs and conduct research on this human rights activist. They might read the article in the *New Yorker* "Zimbabwe's Powerful Music of Struggle" (Dwamena, 2018) and relate it to current activism music in the United States.

Similarly, students can listen to and analyze the lyrics of the Bob Marley song "Zimbabwe," referenced in the aforementioned article, and write their own poems/songs related to the social justice topic of their choice or connected to topics developed in the book. Teachers might also have students listen to (or read the transcripts of) the NPR segment "Two Different Musical Takes on Politics in Zimbabwe" (2005) and compare the scenes each depicts, perhaps even creating images from each song to hang in the classroom.

Throughout the book, Martin describes life in his Zimbabwe home. He says:

> Zimbabwe was in a full-fledged economic crisis: there were riots in Harare and Bulawayo—the government called in the army after people started smashing windows at grocery stores. Their reasoning was "since we cannot afford to buy bread, then we must just take it." People were arrested or beaten as a result. A few even died, trampled or shot by police. . . . Hunger makes people act crazy. I even witnessed one man knifing another for cutting in line to buy bread. (p. 61)

Teachers can have students consider that line "hunger makes people act crazy" and analyze its meaning, providing examples from history, current events, literature, and film. In doing so they can begin to untangle the complexity of poverty in developing countries as they consider questions like *What role does/should the government have in providing food support to those in need?*

As a connected example regarding another developing country, Haiti, people from the United States often go to developing countries to adopt children in orphanages. However, "Of the roughly 30,000 children in Haitian institutions and the hundreds adopted by foreigners each year, the Haitian government estimates that 80% have at least one living parent" (Mauren & Miller, 2016).

Students can contemplate why parents might send their children to an orphanage, and what might be an alternative solution to having people from other countries adopt these children who already have parents. Reflecting on Martin's life, *What might lead his parents or the parents of his classmates, or later, his own students, to take their children to an orphanage? What were the supports and resources his family needed the most?* Students can track the resources and supports that Caitlin and her family provided Martin and his family, and brainstorm other ways that Martin's family might have been able to receive this kind of support that, quite literally, saved the family's life. They might also research the practice of adoption abroad, identifying and debating both sides of this controversial issue.

Throughout the book, Martin is desperate for education. This might be a strange concept for students, so teachers can help them to identify *Why do you think education is so important to Martin? Why do many students in the United States NOT want to go to school? What are the barriers to education that Martin faces? How much does it cost to go to school, and what else is needed besides the fees in order to go to school? What are the tests like? How does Martin reach his ultimate goal of completing college? What do you think is the value of education to people in developing nations as compared to the value of education to people in the United States? Why?*

After Reading

Stories about developing countries rarely make the headlines in US news. Students might want to follow some international news sources (e.g., BBC News) and track the news stories about developing nations. Often, when news stories regarding people from developing countries do make the local news, it is negative and panic inducing (e.g., stories about Ebola and Zika). Students can track US news stories about people from developing countries and compare those with news stories about developing countries provided from international news sources such as the BBC. They can analyze the visuals that accompany those stories and draw conclusions regarding how people from developing countries are depicted, speculate why that might be, and identify the repercussions of such representations.

Caitlin's mom spends a great deal of time trying to find a college that will be a good fit for Martin, even bringing the family dog to campus to see how students respond to her. She explains that since Martin's hometown, Nyanga, "is so rural, it does not even register on the map. And don't forget, Martin, no matter how intelligent, did not own shoes until six months ago. We have to pick carefully" (p. 298).

There are a variety of types of colleges in the United States—small, large, rural, suburban, land grant, public, and private—and each has its own strengths. Additionally, a four-year institution is not the only option students have, as evidenced in the book with Caitlin enrolling in community college. Students can consider their own postsecondary options. Whether they plan on going straight into the workforce, joining the military, or attending community or a four-year college, there are many factors to consider as well as potential barriers to overcome.

Students can identify these potential barriers and develop plans to surpass them. They can consider aspects of a job, career, college, and more that are the most important to them as well as those that have a lesser priority. If possible, teachers can invite career and college counselors into the class as well as people from different professions, and students can create their own postsecondary education plans and calendars.

In conjunction with planning for his own educational future, Martin attends a "pre-departure orientation for Zimbabwean students who were planning to study in America" (p. 346) at the US embassy. The orientation "was to prepare us for some of the bigger cultural differences between Zimbabwe and America" (p. 348).

In addition to topics like US currency, food, and clothing, the Zimbabwean students learn about some customs that they will most likely encounter on campus. For example, "If you have a roommate, you don't have to offer them any of your food. . . . And if your roommate leaves food in the fridge, you have to ask permission before you eat it" (p. 348). These are strange and ridiculous concepts to the Zimbabwean students. Similarly, they are told, "If someone asks, 'How's it going?' The answer to that question is 'Fine.' . . . No one has time for anything else" (p. 350).

Teachers can facilitate a discussion regarding these and other cultural lessons the students from Zimbabwe learn, posing questions like *Do you think these statements are true? Are they important lessons to be taught? What else should students from another culture know before coming to the United States in general or to your high school in particular? Why do you think these differences in cultures exist? What does it say about each culture's priorities? What can we learn from this?*

Finally, the book offers discussion questions after the Epilogue that can be used throughout the reading of the book, and likewise, students might want to join the *I Will Always Write Back* Facebook page and/or follow the Twitter account in order to gain more information about Caitlin, Martin, and all who have read and love their book.

IDEAS FOR SOCIAL ACTION

Caitlin tries to join the African American Awareness Club and the Break Dance Clubs at her school, neither of which goes well for her. Students can discuss *Why do you think Caitlin tried to join these clubs? Why do you think she didn't fit in?* Students then can identify the clubs that exist in their own school and analyze their effectiveness at inclusivity. *Are there membership requirements? Should there be? What is the purpose of these clubs? How can excluding/including certain people and or groups strengthen and/or weaken the club's mission?* If students identify a club that is lacking, they can, perhaps, begin work on creating that club for their own school.

In the Epilogue of the book, Caitlin and Martin explain why they wrote the book/shared their story. Caitlin says, "If we can inspire just one person to do something kind, we will have done enough" (p. 390). Later she says, "If our story could move people to tears, could it move them to act? . . . To be kinder to one another? . . . To take a chance and do good things for deserving people?" (p. 391). Students can brainstorm ways, both large and small, that they can be kinder to others and "do good things" for those in need.

For a larger-scale project idea, Poverty Resolutions (2018) offers suggestions for developing a Poverty Week in individual communities as part of an awareness campaign and in an effort to help combat poverty and support those in need. Students can access the Poverty Resolutions website in order to get ideas regarding how they might conduct their own Poverty Week in their school and/or local community.

In unpacking the complexity of extreme poverty in developing countries, teachers can lead students in understanding that simply "giving" is not enough, and, in fact, can do more harm than good. Students can research NGOs that are positively impacting people in developing countries by focusing on providing agency and opportunities to individuals in their own communities. They can identify locations where people can support the sustainable trade system through purchasing fair-trade products, be it in their communities or online. Using this information, students can lead an awareness campaign, creating brochures or websites of NGOs and businesses they feel are worthy of supporting and sharing the goods and services those organizations provide as well as the ways in which to access and support them.

Students can also choose a specific community in a developing country, identify the needs of that community, and then brainstorm actions to support those needs in ways that empower and offer agency for the members who live there. A unit of study on global poverty may inspire students to consider the needs of others—around the world as well as in their own communities—and encourage them to consider the ways in which *they* can make a positive impact at both individual and systemic levels.

SUPPLEMENTAL RESOURCES

Canonical Companions

Things Fall Apart by Chinua Achebe
A Thousand Splendid Suns by Khaled Hosseini
Les Miserables by Victor Hugo
Annie John by Jamaica Kincaid
Angela's Ashes by Frank McCourt
"A Modest Proposal" by Jonathan Swift

Connected Young Adult Literature

City of Saints & Thieves by Natalie C. Anderson
Serafina's Promise by Ann E. Burg
In Darkness by Nick Lake
The Milk of Birds by Sylvia Whitman

Connected Music

"Larger Than Life" by the Backstreet Boys

"Who Let the Dogs Out" by Baha Men
"Do They Know It's Christmas" by Band Aid 30
"Zimbabwe" by Bob Marley
"The Real Slim Shady" by Eminem
"Most Girls" by P!nk
"Living la Vida Loca" by Ricky Martin
Any songs by Thomas Mapfumo
Any songs from the Rolling Stones, Cream, and/or Led Zeppelin
"Wannabe" and "Viva Forever" by the Spice Girls

REFERENCES

Alifirenka, C. & Ganda, M. (2015). *I will always write back.* New York: Little, Brown.

Cobb, C. & Leblanc, C. (Producers), & Diaz, P. (Director). (2009). *The end of poverty?* [Documentary]. United States: Cinema Libre Studio.

Dwamena, A. (March 2018). Zimbabwe's powerful music of struggle. *The New Yorker.* Retrieved from https://www.newyorker.com/culture/culture-desk/zimbabwes-powerful-music-of-struggle.

Hambouz, A. & Eisenhauer, Y. C. (2006). Feeling vulnerable. The Learning Network: Teaching and Learning with the *New York Times.* Retrieved from https://learning.blogs.nytimes.com/2006/03/14/feeling-vulnerable/.

Martin, W. (2018, June 1). Ranked: The 28 poorest countries in the world—where people live on less than $1,000 per year. *Business Insider.* Retrieved from https://nordic.businessinsider.com/poorest-countries-in-the-world-2018-5.

Mauren, K. (Producer) & Miller, M. M. (Director). (2016). *Poverty, Inc.* [Documentary]. United States: Brainstorm Media.

Mussman, J. (Producer) & Roth, V. (Director). (2017). *Daughters of destiny* [Docuseries]. United States: Cause & Affect Media.

NPR. (2005). Two different musical takes on politics in Zimbabwe. Retrieved from https://www.npr.org/templates/transcript/transcript.php?storyId=4750457.

Poverty Resolutions. (2018). Poverty week. Retrieved from http://povertyresolutions.org/povertyweek/index.php.

Raptim. (2018). 45 organizations that battle poverty. Retrieved from https://www.raptim.org/45-organizations-that-battle-poverty/.

Roser, M. & Ortiz-Ospina, E. (2017). Global extreme poverty. Retrieved from https://ourworldindata.org/extreme-poverty.

Teaching Tolerance. (1991–2018). Retrieved from https://www.tolerance.org/classroom-resources/tolerance-lessons/education-evaluation.

United Nations. (2003). International bill of human rights. Retrieved from https://www.ohchr.org/documents/publications/compilation1.1en.pdf.

United Nations. (n.d.). Sustainable development goals. Retrieved from https://www.un.org/sustainabledevelopment/sustainable-development-goals/.

The World Bank. (2018). Poverty and equity data portal. Retrieved from http://povertydata.worldbank.org/poverty/home/.

3

MENTAL HEALTH

According to the National Alliance on Mental Illness, "one in five children ages 13–18 has or will have a serious mental illness." Moreover, suicide is the third leading cause of death among young people between the ages of ten and twenty-four, with 90 percent of those who have died by suicide "having an underlying mental illness" (National Alliance on Mental Illness, n.d., para. 3). There are a variety of illnesses that fall under the category of mental health.

The most common mental illnesses for young adults "include those related to anxiety, depression, attention deficit-hyperactivity, and eating" (US Department of Health, n.d., para. 1). Recent studies show that the most common mental health disorder in adolescents is anxiety disorder (nearly 32 percent of teens) followed by depression, "which affects nearly one in eight (12.5%) adolescents and young adults each year" (US Department of Health, n.d., para. 3, 6, 9).

To exacerbate the problem, whether it is lack of access to care, lack of reporting, or other reasons, teens largely are not getting treatment for their mental health challenges. According to the National Center for Children in Poverty (NCCP): "Among adolescents with mental health needs, 70% do not receive needed care" (NCCP, 2018, para. 20). This is especially problematic as "mental health problems may lead to poor school performance, school dropout, strained family relationships, involvement with the child welfare or juvenile justice systems, substance abuse, and engaging in risky sexual behaviors" (NCCP, 2018, para. 15).

Unfortunately, there is still a stigma surrounding mental illness. Those who live with mental illness are often blamed, teased, or not believed. According to the National Alliance on Mental Illness:

> Most people who live with mental illness have, at some point, been blamed for their condition. They've been called names. Their symptoms have been referred to as "a phase" or something they can control "if they only tried." They have been illegally discriminated against, with no justice. . . . Stigma causes people to feel ashamed for something that is out of their control. Worst of all, stigma prevents people from seeking the help they need. (Greenstein, 2017, para. 1–2)

There are a variety of ways to combat the stigmas surrounding mental illness, including "talk(ing) openly about mental health, educate(ing) yourself and others, and be(ing) conscious of language" (Greenstein, 2017, para. 4–6).

It is crucial that mental health education take place in K–12 schools, and the health classroom is not the only place where the work can be done. In reading and discussing literature that portrays characters with mental illness, teachers can begin to fight the stigmas and help those students who have mental health challenges feel more accepted and comfortable in seeking the help and support they need.

In this chapter, we focus on the topic of mental health. With the prevalence of mental illness in teens, the stigmas surrounding mental illness, and the potentially devastating consequences of leaving mental health challenges untreated, it is important that students gain comfort in engaging with the topic of mental wellness, and YA literature can provide a vehicle by which to begin.

THE UNLIKELY HERO OF ROOM 13B

With the majority of the characters displaying symptoms of mental illness, Teresa Toten's (2013) *The Unlikely Hero of Room 13B* has a clear focus on mental health, though it is, above all, a love story. The novel largely takes place during various sessions of an Obsessive Compulsive Disorder (OCD) support group for adolescents, and as the plot unfolds it is revealed that, while mental illness is one (often encompassing) component of the characters depicted, they are all so much more than their diagnoses and symptoms. They desire and deserve love, friendships, happiness, and good health, and should not be feared or ridiculed for their mental health challenges.

The protagonist of the novel is Adam. Known in his therapy group as "Batman," Adam falls head over heels in love with Robyn ("Robin"), who also attends the OCD support group meetings. Adam's illness presents itself through various compulsions, including his need for counting, tapping, and magical thinking regarding thresholds. He parents are divorced, and though he lives primarily with his mother, who exhibits her own mental health challenges, including hoarding and culminating in a complete psychotic break, he also spends time in the home of his father; his father's new wife, Brenda; and their son Wendell "Sweetie," who shows signs of extreme anxiety that only Adam seems to be able to calm.

As the book progresses, the reader gets to know the various participants in the OCD support group, watch the development of a relationship between Adam and Robin, and vicariously experience Adam's struggle with wanting to feel better and not being able to control his mental health to his satisfaction. The book ends with a feeling of hope—that despite major setbacks, with proper attention, therapy, and medication, the various characters' mental illnesses will be managed such that the characters can live fulfilling lives.

We chose this book not only because it is an engaging story with relatable characters the reader will root for, but also because misconceptions about OCD abound. The term *OCD* seems to be used widely and inappropriately, with people who like things neat and orderly often describing themselves as OCD. This oversimplification and overuse of the term negates the severity of this illness and the paralyzing effects it can have on the lives of those who live with it.

As such, while there are numerous YA novels that honestly and accurately describe living with mental illness in life-affirming ways (see Connected YA Literature list), we chose this book to highlight a lesser-talked-about illness and the good that can come from finding the right combination of therapy, medication, and support for those struggling with their own mental health.

TEACHING STRATEGIES

Before Reading

There are multiple websites that offer lesson plans and activities to help students better understand mental illness and the challenges and stigmas surrounding those who struggle with their mental health. For example, the Canadian "Can We Talk" website shares lesson plans and activities geared toward introducing students to terms associated with mental health, reducing stigmas surrounding mental illness, and helping students increase awareness regarding their personal mental wellness.

Lesson #2 on the site offers a "Personal Attitude Survey" for students to complete in order to identify their own beliefs and opinions about mental illness. The survey contains questions like, "Females are more likely to have a mental illness than males" and "People with mental illness are generally violent and dangerous" (Can We Talk, n.d., p. 7).

One of the activities regarding the survey suggests teachers have students complete the survey on their own and then, through a show of hands, share their answers with the whole class while the teacher tallies the students' responses. However, we suggest not having a whole class sharing of answers, as that can be uncomfortable for students. Instead, they can anonymously submit their responses or, if teachers have access to classroom clicker technology (e.g., Kahoot, Acadly, iClickers), they can implement it in order to gather student responses while keeping their anonymity.

The topic of mental illness, as well as fostering and nurturing one's own mental wellness, offers opportunities for teachers to incorporate related nonfiction texts into the classroom as well. For example, Tori Rodriguez's (2015) article "Teenagers Who Don't Get Enough Sleep at Higher Risk for Mental Health Problems" allows students to consider their own healthy practices. They can track the amount of sleep they are getting, track the ways in which they are spending their time after school, and identify ways in which they might be able to get more sleep into their daily routine.

Activities like these focus on control and management of one's own life. While getting more sleep, eating more healthily, and getting more exercise will not necessarily cure mental illness, those activities can help to manage symptoms, and helping students to make healthy life decisions can easily be included into the classroom, regardless of content area.

Similarly, the article "Coping Mechanisms" by the CommonLit Staff (2016) provides students with concrete ways in which to deal with stress in their lives. Teachers can prompt students to try each of the coping mechanisms identified in the article and to journal about how or if each worked for them. Incorporating articles and activities like these into the English classroom can help to send the message that personal wellness is a topic that spans the curriculum and is not just to be considered in health class.

There is a series of CGI (computer-generated imagery) animated short films that share experiences with different types of mental illness, from Alzheimer's and dementia to anxiety, depression, bipolar disorder, schizoaffective disorder, OCD, and addiction. These short (six- to eleven-minute) films are easily accessible and offer insight into mental illness in an engaging way (Shahanand, 2016).

Before reading the novel, for example, teachers can show the animated short "Out of Bounds" to offer one example of OCD. Students can then identify what challenges OCD presents to the main character of this film as well as how he tries to manage his symptoms in order to protect his pet fish (The Animation Workshop, 2014).

Another animated short, "Tzadik," is a six-minute film that personifies depression and the perpetual struggle to escape it (Berkovits, 2014), and "In Between" is a three-minute animated short depicting anxiety (Gobelins, 2012). Teachers can introduce a unit of study on mental wellness by showing these clips, followed by other personifications of mental health in literature and film.

For example, throughout the Harry Potter books and films, Dementors appear, "shaped like humans covered in dark hooded cloaks. . . . Though they are blind, they can sense and feed on positive feelings, draining their victim's happiness" (Pottermore, n.d., para. 1). Author J. K. Rowling explains, "If it can, the Dementor will feed on you long enough to reduce you to something like itself . . . soulless and evil. You'll be left with nothing but the worst experiences of your life." Dementors "freeze your insides" and, most importantly, "they don't need walls" to keep their prisoners, their prisoners become "trapped inside their own heads" (Entwistle, 2016, para. 20).

In an interview in 2000, J. K. Rowling confirmed that the Dementors in her Harry Potter series are a symbol for depression:

> It was entirely conscious. And entirely from my own experience. Depression is the most unpleasant thing I have ever experienced. It is that absence of being able to envisage that you will ever be cheerful again. The absence of hope. That very deadened feeling, which is so very different from feeling sad. Sad hurts but it's a healthy feeling. It's a necessary thing to feel. Depression is very different. (White, 2016, para. 1)

Teachers can share clips of the Dementors from the Harry Potter movies to compare with the CGI animated shorts mentioned above, comparing the various personified representations of mental illness, and by using a graphic organizer such as a Venn diagram to identify similarities and differences. Following, students can brainstorm how they might personify other emotions (e.g., joy, surprise, fear) and/or illnesses (e.g., chronic, mental, common every day), creating a character sketch, comic strip, short story, or poem to share their representations.

During Reading

Throughout the novel *The Unlikely Hero of Room 13B*, the teens in the OCD support group use words like *nuts* and *whack* to describe themselves. Teachers can write these words on the board as readers encounter them and have students keep a running list of both denotations and connotations for the identified words. After reading, teachers can direct students to do the same for the word *normal*. An analysis of rhetoric and what effects word choice can have on people's perceptions of themselves and others can follow, with students identifying other words they can use when talking about people who struggle with mental illness.

Also in the novel, each member of the support group chooses a name to be their alter ego. The characters end up choosing names of superheroes and reality stars. Teachers can have their students choose their own alter ego and write narratives regarding their personal stories—how the chosen alter ego represents aspects they possess as well as qualities they would like to emulate. The narratives can be written in traditional style, or students can choose to create a comic strip/graphic novel version to share with the class and/or in the school's literary magazine, newspaper, newsletter, or class website.

There are a multitude of artists who have explored the topic of mental illness through their music. For example, in his song "1-800-273-8255," hip-hop artist Logic talks about his struggle with depression and suicide with an uplifting message. Teachers can first have students read the lyrics and speculate what the phone number, the title of the song, is (The National Suicide Prevention Lifeline). Then they can consider what the song is about, and why, perhaps, Logic wrote it. Teachers might then share Logic's own explanation. He writes:

> And then it hit me, the power that I have as an artist with a voice. I wasn't even trying to save your life. Now what can happen if I actually did? And it's beyond just this song. It's the whole album. What can happen if I took myself out of my comfort zone and made a whole album about everybody and everybody's struggles including my own which is one I've never done. What if I silenced my own fear and I say, "I'm scared to talk about my race. I'm scared to talk about the state of this country but I'm going to do it anyway. I'm going to persevere. Man, how many lives can I really save then?" (Logic, 2018, para. 3)

Students can consider the power artists have and the power they, too, have in sharing their stories. They can discuss what putting songs and stories like this into the public can mean for breaking down stigmas and helping others to not feel so alone in their struggles, whatever they may be.

Students might then read the article "Hip Hop Works to Break Down Mental Health Stigma for Black Men" (Taylor, 2017) and consider why stigmas may be stronger for certain groups of people (race, ethnicity, gender, sexuality, economic, ability). Following this discussion, students can identify other stigmas surrounding particular groups of people and consider ways in which to break down existing stigmas and support the health and well-being of all.

Other artists have also written about mental health, and the lyrics of these songs can similarly be analyzed. We caution teachers, however, to be judicious in their song selection. While many artists have written about their personal experiences with mental illness, we feel strongly that teens, as an especially vulnerable population, need songs that offer, along with honest depictions of mental health, a message of hope—that the lives of teens are valuable, that they are not alone, and that we believe they can fight.

With this in mind, teachers can choose songs that have powerful messages and lead students in creating posters, perhaps citing some of those uplifting lyrics, and hanging them up around school and/or in the community. Rachel Platten's "Fight Song," Jessie J's "Who You Are," Paramore's "Last Hope," Florence and the Machine's "Shake It Out," and We the Kings' "Just Keep Breathing" are some examples of songs that have been interpreted as being connected to mental illness and that offer a message of hope.

Finally, as part of his therapy, Adam (Batman) is supposed to make lists of what he believes. Students can follow this format, creating their own personal belief lists. From the lists, and inspired by other poetry and song lyrics they have read, students can create their own poems. If they are struggling with format, Found Poems can be a good place to start. Or, if they want to work with a partner, Poems in Two Voices is a powerful format that allows for a performance component as well. Teachers can lead students in discussing why it is a valuable practice to identify their own beliefs and, moreover, to share those beliefs with others.

After Reading

There are a variety of topics that students might want to research regarding various aspects of mental health. For example, students can research the history of the treatment of people with mental illness in the United States, investigating the practice of institutionalization and the progression of medical procedures and treatments used throughout the years.

Or, students might want to choose one particular mental illness and research it specifically. Depression, self-harm, suicide ideation, eating disorders, and substance abuse are highly prevalent among adolescents. In choosing a particular mental illness to research and then sharing findings with the class via gallery walk, multimedia presentation, or oral report, all students may better understand definitions of and signs, symptoms, and treatments for various illnesses, thereby demystifying the diseases and debunking stereotypes and stigmas that surround those who struggle with mental health.

Similarly, students can research famous people who struggle with mental illness, highlighting their successes and thereby demonstrating that it is possible to have a full, productive life with mental illness, as long as help is procured to manage the symptoms.

Students can share the person they researched (e.g., Dwayne "The Rock" Johnson, Frida Kahlo, Mary Todd Lincoln, Demi Lovato, Isaac Newton, Michael Phelps) with the class through a wax museum biography research report exhibit, where the students dress up like the person researched and stand silently in front of backdrops they created that share information about the person they are representing. "Wax Museum visitors (parents and the other kids from . . . school) walk around, looking at the famous people and pushing the button on the backdrop, to hear the child tell them a little bit about his/her life and why he/she is important" (Larson, 2015).

Marcel "Fable the Poet" Price is "an official partner of Mental Health America," advocating for the importance of mental health awareness among children and teens. He has written several poems about his struggles with mental wellness. For example, his first book, *Adrift in a Sea of M&Ms*, he published "to help individuals battling with mental wellness, and the stressors that come along with being a person of color in America" (Price, 2017, para. 13). Teachers can show a brief video introducing Fable the Poet (Flinn Foundation, 2017) and then have students read or watch him read some of his poems, analyzing them for not only their messages but also the literary techniques employed.

In addition to Marcel Price's poems, teachers can also go to the poets.org website to access poems recommended for teens "about anxiety, depression, and other mental health issues, as well as poems about hope, resilience, and survival" (Academy of American Poets, 2017), like Emily Dickinson's "The Soul Has Bandaged Moments," Naomi Shihab Nye's "The Rider," and Judith Viorst's "Fifteen, Maybe Sixteen Things to Worry About." After reading several different poems regarding mental wellness, students might compose their own poems, modeling those they have read from the perspectives of different characters in the novel.

IDEAS FOR SOCIAL ACTION

As part of an awareness campaign, students might want to research representations of mental illness in film and television, identifying examples where stereotypes are reified as well as identifying honest, life-affirming portrayals. Students can sponsor a viewing of one of the films they have researched, and, before or after the film, lead a discussion with the audience, sharing statistics regarding mental illness, stereotypes and stigmas, and resources for where to get help.

The Perspective Project "hosts art, poetry and writing with the aim of ending stigma and providing an outlet for those with mental health problems" (*The Guardian Weekly*, 2018, para. 1). Teachers can introduce students to the Perspective Project, perhaps first by having them analyze some of the artwork included (*The Guardian Weekly*, 2018). Afterward, students can use the Perspective Project as a model and inspiration for their own project that aims to reduce stigma surrounding mental illness, soliciting anonymous artwork, photography, and writing, then hosting a gallery event for the community.

In the novel *The Unlikely Hero of Room 13B*, in addition to Adam's own health, he struggles with how to manage his mother's mental illness. He is unsure of what, if anything, he should do or say. His mother has asked him to stay silent, but he is worried that she is sick and will cause harm to herself.

Having a parent, caretaker, or family member who is mentally ill can be scary. Students might want to make a handbook of resources for children who find themselves worried about their parents' or caretakers' mental health. With "do"s and "don't"s, like when and whom to tell, and how to ask for help, written in child-friendly language and formats, a resource like this can be shared with children at the elementary school. Skits of scenarios could also be performed to educate children of what they can do, what they can say, and where they can go if they want to help a friend and/or find themselves in uncomfortable situations connected to a loved one's mental health.

Also in the novel, the teen OCD support group provides emotional support for the characters in a variety of ways. Teachers can guide students in identifying how to be an active listener and potential ways in which to respond to their peers in need. Similar to the skits mentioned above, or maybe in conjunction with them, students can create positive and negative active listening examples that they can perform for elementary and/or middle school students, followed by discussion on why it is important to be an active listener and a good friend to all of their classmates.

With such a prevalence of mental illness in our nation today, it is likely that students will either know someone or be personally affected by challenges surrounding mental health. Activities like the ones mentioned above can help students to take some control of this life-threatening illness for which they may feel powerless by changing the narrative, helping to eradicate the stigma, and sharing stories of resilience that can provide hope for those in need.

SUPPLEMENTAL RESOURCES

Canonical Companions

The Awakening by Kate Chopin
The Yellow Wallpaper by Charlotte Perkins Gilman
Beloved by Toni Morrison
Hamlet by William Shakespeare

Connected Young Adult Literature

Wintergirls by Laurie Halse Anderson
13 Reasons Why by Jay Asher
The Perks of Being a Wallflower by Stephen Chbosky
Girl in Pieces by Kathleen Glasgow
Turtles All the Way Down by John Green
All the Bright Places by Jennifer Niven
Challenger Deep by Neal Shusterman

Connected Music

"Shake It Out" by Florence and the Machine
"Who You Are" by Jessie J
"1-800-273-8255" by Logic

"Last Hope" by Paramore

"Fight Song" by Rachel Platten

"Just Keep Breathing" by We the Kings

REFERENCES

Academy of American Poets. (2017). Mental health: Poems for teens. Retrieved from https://www.poets.org/poetsorg/text/mental-health-poems-teens.

The Animation Workshop. (2014). Out of bounds. Retrieved from https://youtu.be/cI2Zwr68B-k.

Berkovits, O. (2014). Tzadik. Retrieved from https://youtu.be/gW1x51zezqE.

Can We Talk. (n.d.). Mental health lesson plans. Retrieved from http://canwetalk.ca/wp-content/uploads/2016/03/COOR-79l-2016-03-CWT-lesson-plans.pdf.

CommonLit Staff. (2016). Coping mechanisms. Retrieved from https://www.commonlit.org/texts/coping-mechanisms.

Entwistle, L. (2016). Depression and dementors: The magic of Harry Potter and grief. Retrieved from https://medium.com/@lauren_victoria/depression-and-dementors-the-wonder-of-harry-potter-and-grief-40295fc7cbf7.

Flinn Foundation. (2017). Fable the poet: Opening minds ending stigma. Retrieved from https://www.youtube.com/watch?v=ROS6vGEEhl4.

Gobelins. (2012). *In between—Animated short films.* Retrieved from https://youtu.be/2xp22IYL2uU.

Greenstein, L. (2017). 9 ways to fight mental health stigma. Retrieved from https://www.nami.org/Blogs/NAMI-Blog/October-2017/9-Ways-to-Fight-Mental-Health-Stigma.

The Guardian Weekly. (2018, January 17). Mental health: Behind the label. Retrieved from https://www.theguardian.com/healthcare-network/gallery/2018/jan/17/eight-artworks-inspired-mental-health-problems-pictures.

Larson, J. (2015). Wax museum: Biography research report and event. Retrieved from https://the-teacher-next-door.com/my-blog/classroom-ideas/wax-museum-biography-research-report-and-event?highlight=WyJ3YXgiLCJtdXNldW0iLCJ3YXggbXVzZXVtIl0=.

Logic. (2018). 1-800-273-8255: What is this song about? Retrieved from https://genius.com/Logic-1-800-273-8255-lyrics.

National Alliance on Mental Illness. (n.d.). Mental health facts: Children and teens. Retrieved from https://www.nami.org/NAMI/media/NAMI-Media/Infographics/Children-MH-Facts-NAMI.pdf.

NCCP: National Center for Children in Poverty. 2018. Adolescent mental health in the United States. Retrieved from http://www.nccp.org/publications/pub_878.html.

Pottermore. (n.d.). Dementors. Retrieved from https://www.pottermore.com/explore-the-story/dementors.

Price, M. (2017). The power of spoken word. Mental Health America. Retrieved from http://www.mentalhealthamerica.net/blog/power-spoken-word.

Rodriguez, T. (2015). Teenagers who don't get enough sleep at higher risk for mental health problems. *Scientific American.* Retrieved from https://www.scientificamerican.com/article/teenagers-who-don-t-get-enough-sleep-at-higher-risk-for-mental-health-problems/.

Shahanand, P. (2016, April 9). 10 beautiful animated short films that show mental disorders in the most subtle way. *Storypick.* Retrieved from https://www.storypick.com/mental-disorder-short-films/.

Taylor, K. (2017). Hip hop works to break down mental health stigma for black men. *NBC News.* Retrieved from https://www.nbcnews.com/pop-culture/music/hip-hop-works-break-down-mental-health-stigma-black-men-n819461.

Toten, T. (2013). *The unlikely hero of room 13B.* New York: Ember.

United States Department of Health and Human Service. (n.d.). Adolescent mental health
    basics. Retrieved from https://www.hhs.gov/ash/oah/adolescent-development/mental-
    health/adolescent-mental-health-basics/common-disorders/index.html.
White, H. (2016). 22 J. K. Rowling facts that prove she is actually a magical human. Retrieved
    from https://www.popsugar.com/tech/photo-gallery/41180052/image/41180427/Rowling-
    created-Dementors-metaphor-depression.

4

THE GENDER SPECTRUM

The gender binary, or the rigid, structural separation of what is traditionally considered masculine or feminine, is pervasive in our society. Clothing stores contain separate sections according to gender; roles and personality traits are often ascribed to individuals by gender (e.g., men are leaders, women are nice); bathrooms are generally marked for women and men.

Gender, however, is not a natural or given aspect of a person. It is rather a social categorization and is different from *sex* in that the former refers to "the collection of characteristics that are culturally associated with maleness or femaleness" while the latter is a "biological term dividing a species into male or female, usually on the basis of chromosomes" ("Terms and Definitions," 2018). Gender exists along a spectrum, and a person's gender identity, then, is their own sense of who they are in terms of man, woman, neither, or both. Many people do not ascribe to the dichotomy of man or woman, rather identifying as, for example, *gender-queer*, *two spirit*, or *agender*. In addition, some do not feel as if their assigned sex at birth matches their gender identity and expression and identify as *transgender*.

The number of people who distinguish themselves along the gender spectrum, however, is difficult to determine. This is due to several reasons: Statistics about gender and sexuality are conflated; terminology related to these communities is ever-changing and complicated; individuals often do not self-report their status as transgender due to safety concerns; and, perhaps even most outstanding, "the US Census and other official records kept by such agencies as the National Archives or state departments of motor vehicles report sex, typically based on the sex assigned at birth or the legal sex, but they do not report current gender identity" (Meerwijk & Sevelius, 2017). Nonetheless, it is estimated that 1.4 million Americans are transgender with "younger adults ages 18 to 24" being more likely to identify as transgender (Hoffman, 2016, para. 5). Furthermore, Herman, Flores, Brown, Wilson, and Conron (2017) drew on state-administered surveys to estimate that 0.7 percent of youth ages thirteen to seventeen, or 150,000 youth, are transgender.

People who do not conform to traditional gender expectations have garnered the public's attention, particularly in popular media through the rise of figures such as Caitlyn Jenner, Laverne Cox, Chaz Bono, and Jazz Jennings. These individuals have received both backlash and support, often under scrutiny as they began living their authentic gender while in the public eye. In the political realm, "Bathroom Bills" have been introduced, which are pieces of legislation that attempt to force people to utilize restrooms that match the sex to which they were assigned at birth rather than potentially that which matches their gender identity. Such policies received massive criticism in states such as North Carolina and Texas where they were introduced.

Furthermore, although the Obama administration protected the rights of transgender individuals in educational institutions under Title IX (Holden, 2018), the Trump administration revoked this ordinance in 2017 (Davis, 2017). While there are not currently any states with existing Bathroom Bills, sixteen states have deliberated on legislation related to gender-segregated facilities; six have entertained prohibiting antidiscrimination laws; and fourteen have "considered legislation that would limit transgender students' rights at school" (Kralik, 2017, para. 4). Thus, "the introduction of such policies, the public support they have garnered, and the federal government's reaction is threatening to LGBTQ+ populations at large" (Jeffries & Boyd, 2018, p. 33).

Harmful policies and damaging attitudes toward transgender and gender-variant youth have serious consequences. In a national survey administered by the Gay, Lesbian and Straight Education Network, 90 percent of transgender students reported "hearing negative remarks about someone's gender expression sometimes, often, or frequently in school" (Greytak, Kosciw, & Diaz, 2009, p. x), and "about two-thirds (65%) of transgender students felt unsafe because of how they expressed their gender" (p. xi). Furthermore, the National Center for Transgender Equality notes of transgender youth:

> Rather than focusing on their education, many students struggle for the ability to come to school and be themselves without being punished for wearing clothes or using facilities consistent with who they are. Some are denied opportunities to go on field trips or participate in sports. Together with bullying and victim-blaming, these conflicts can lead to disproportionate discipline, school pushout, and involvement in the juvenile justice system. ("Youth and Students," 2018, para. 3)

With such evidence of mistreatment and intolerance, it is imperative that teachers address the gender spectrum in schools and create inclusive spaces and respect for the diversity of all students. While gender is often a taken-for-granted aspect of a person, teachers can help to disrupt the normalization of gender expectations in classrooms through reading narratives that exemplify gender variance and can explore how gender non-conformity is often met with social oppression. In this chapter, we focus on Anna-Marie McLemore's (2016) novel *When the Moon Was Ours* to propose methods for introducing, understanding, and studying the gender spectrum and for working with students to disrupt related ignorance and prejudice, promoting positive perspectives on the myriad manifestations that gender can assume.

WHEN THE MOON WAS OURS

Interweaving elements of magical realism with plot and character development, *When the Moon Was Ours* is a novel featuring two friends, Miel and Sam, who develop an intense relationship as they navigate their society, peers, and family relationships. Miel, who emerged one day from out of the town's water tower at age five, struggles to understand her family history and the significance of the roses that grow from her arm.

Bullied by the Bonner sisters, four adolescent females known for their mystic beauty and sly actions, Miel finds the strength to stand up for herself and her friend, Sam. As the novel progresses, readers learn that Sam, born Samira, follows the Pakistani custom of *bacha posh* in which young women dress and conduct themselves as boys until they become adults. Sam explains that he does this "so that he could take care of his mother, so there would be a man of the house even though his mother had no sons" (p. 34).

According to custom, Sam would eventually return to living as a woman and become a wife. Sam, however, actually identifies as a man and wants to remain living as such. He thus struggles in the novel with telling his mother about his authentic gender identity. While very few people in the town know Sam's story, he reveals himself to Miel and the two engage in a romantic relationship. Miel protects Sam when the Bonner sisters threaten to disclose his secret after Miel refuses to surrender her roses to them.

Readers later learn that Sam is not the only transgender character in the novel but that Miel's brother, who she thought died at a young age, was magically transitioned in the water to Aracely, the woman who becomes Miel's caretaker after she arrives in town. Aracely offers an adult perspective on being transgender, telling Sam, "We don't get to become who we are for nothing. It costs something" (p. 155). We chose this book therefore because it raises issues related to gender, including self-identification, access to facilities, and social acceptance.

TEACHING STRATEGIES

Before Reading

Prior to approaching the novel, teachers would likely find it helpful for students to start with a brief overview of magical realism as a genre of writing. Often characteristic of writers from Latin America, "the magical realist creates a new reality. This is characterized by the matter-of-fact inclusion of fantastic or magical elements into seemingly realistic fiction" (Mattingly, 2013, para. 2). Magical realism requires somewhat of a suspension of disbelief, but not as extensive as in fantasy or science fiction, and thus students who are unfamiliar with the genre may need some scaffolding to fully appreciate its elements.

In order to acquaint students with magical realism and to later draw points of comparison, students could read one of Gabriel García Márquez's short stories, as García Márquez is one of the most well-known magical realists. They could read either "The Handsomest Drowned Man in the World" (García Márquez, 1968) or "A Very Old

Man with Enormous Wings" (García Márquez, 1955), both of which are online, and keep a running log of the realistic and magical elements as they read.

Teachers might ask students in reference to either story: *What aspects of the setting seem like they could exist today? What qualities of the main character are improbable? How does the magical quality add to the story? How does the story require us to use our imagination in ways that are different from traditional fiction?* Students might also view any number of films that reflect magical realism as well, such as *The Shape of Water* (Dale & del Torro, 2018), *Amélie* (Deschamps, Ossard, & Jeunet, 2001), or *Big Fish* (Zanuck, Cohen, Jinks, & Burton, 2003), and answer these same questions.

Beyond this foundation, and given the focus on gender in *When the Moon Was Ours*, teachers will also need to spend time prior to reading establishing students' knowledge of gender as a social construct and working through key terms to use as they discuss the book. As mentioned in the previous section, initially differentiating between sex and gender is key; often these are conflated or the two are expected to match for individuals when that does not have to be the case.

Terms for teachers to include in this discussion (and related to the text) are: *sex, gender, cisgender, transgender, sexual orientation, homophobia, transphobia,* and *gender identity.* The Gay, Lesbian, & Straight Education Network (GLSEN) has excellent resources, including a "Key Concepts and Terms" (2014) document that serves as an outstanding reference for meanings and explanations. Teachers should gauge their own comfort levels with these terms and educate themselves where necessary, as students may ask an array of related questions.

However, this can also be a powerful area of collaborative learning for teachers and students wherein the teacher might model seeking out answers to questions they may not know. Modeling where and how to find resources to learn more about the gender spectrum would be a powerful practice for students to witness, and such actions would show students that acceptance and a willingness to learn are positive traits as there is not an expectation that one person knows everything there is to know about the gender spectrum. Teachers should, nonetheless, emphasize to students that allowing a person to identify themselves is generally best practice, rather than ascribing a label to someone themselves.

To further introduce students to thinking critically about gender, teachers can ask youth to brainstorm common expectations surrounding *man* and *woman*. They might ask groups of students to visually depict answers to the prompts: *What do you think of when you hear the terms* man *and* woman? *What roles and qualities do you envision of each? How is each "supposed" to act?* Once students have completed these drawings, they might then analyze their classmates' in comparison to their own, walking around the room to survey similarities and differences in others' posted artwork. Drawings will likely contain analogous images, and teachers might use these as a springboard to discuss how people develop notions of gender and from where those originate (Roloff & Boyd, 2018).

Teachers could also utilize children's books to further allow students to consider aspects related to being transgender. For instance, *I Am Jazz* (Herthel & Jennings, 2014), based on the real-life experience of Jazz Jennings, describes how Jazz knew at a young age she did not identify as a boy. Similarly, *Red, A Crayon's Story* (Hall, 2015) describes a crayon who feels its color is mistakenly labeled by others. Educators can use these stories as conversation starters, asking students to consider what it might feel like to be mislabeled by others or to feel differently on the inside than how one is perceived on the outside. Students can then transition to reading more advanced narratives, such as some from the nonfiction text *Beyond Magenta* (Kuklin, 2014), which highlights the voices of trans youth who explain their experiences with their gender identities.

As matters surrounding gender are personal, teachers might ask students to journal individually on related questions, giving students options so as not to run the risk of "outing" anyone but soliciting students' critical thoughts on gender. Students could choose from inquiries such as: *How do you identify your gender? When did you know your gender? What are the gender expectations in your family? Why do you think there are different gender expectations for women and men? How does your gender contribute to your identity?* These are wide ranging so that students can choose to either share personal experiences or comment on society, as they are likely still developing their understandings and may not yet wish to apply the critical lens to themselves. Regardless, considering how gender relates to a person's identity is central to understanding the gravity of the gender spectrum—while students may want to easily dismiss "boy" and "girl" identifications as insignificant, it is crucial to help them see that in fact gender does affect a person's identity (internally) and the way they are perceived by others (externally).

Teachers can then give students the option to share their writing based on their chosen journal prompt with the class or in small groups. While some students may not want to share and the teacher should honor that stance, others may choose to disclose their answers to any of the above questions, and this could serve as a potent classroom experience for the development of empathy and establishment of trust prior to reading the novel.

During Reading

A number of allusions arise in the novel that students can research to enhance their background knowledge and to facilitate a better grasp on the characters' lives and the storyline. Teachers can introduce students to the cultural customs that are addressed in the book as they appear and allow students the space to conduct their own research and secure information about those traditions. These include the legend of La Llorona, also known as "The Weeping Woman," which becomes important as students learn about Miel's mother and the various interpretations of her actions. The video explanation, "La Llorona: The Weeping Woman (Urban Legend Explained)" (Mytholgy & Fiction Explained, 2017) on YouTube or the informational text online "La Llorona—Weeping Woman of the Southwest" (Weiser, 2017) are both useful in explaining the assorted versions of the legend.

In addition to this allusion, and since the tradition of bacha posh is introduced early in the novel, students could research the custom when they learn of Sam's grandmother sharing it with him. Sam recounts for readers that his grandmother "had told him the name for these girls. She had brought it with her from Pakistan, and from stories she'd heard from across the border in Afghanistan. Bacha posh. Dressed as a boy. Girls whose parents decided that, until they were grown, they would be sons" (McLemore, 2016, p. 35). Students might research the cultural practice, guided by teachers' questions such as: *How did this tradition originate? Why would parents choose this life for their daughters? What advantages might it give them? Why would a single mother be better off having a son, according to Sam's perspective?*

Students could then teach the class what they learned and engage in conversation about the tradition. They could also extend their knowledge and inquiry through viewing the Netflix animated film *The Breadwinner*, which documents a young Afghan girl's experiences as she disguises herself as a boy in order to secure work and provide for her family. They could compare the girl in the film to Miel and delve deeply into *why* it is that one would conceal their identity in this manner.

As students discuss bacha posh, it will be important that teachers monitor their reactions, attempting to guard against "othering" language or dismissal of the custom as "weird" or "foreign." In order to work toward a more affirming understanding, students might apply the custom to their own contexts and consider the benefits that growing up as a man in the United States would secure for individuals versus growing up a woman. Sam confronts this notion in a conversation with Aracely in the book, asking: "You think girls can do whatever they want here? You think Miel can? How do you think girls here would do if they got to be boys growing up and then had to be girls again?" (McLemore, 2016, p. 97).

Teachers can ask students to consider Sam's questions, further asking: *To what extent would this be similar to the gains received under bacha posh, and to what extent would it be different?* Not only would this prompt further understanding of Pakistani society, but it also would develop students' critical literacies surrounding gender in our own culture. We caution teachers against having students who identify as men consider growing up as women, since the issue is related to power in society and to do so would obscure that aspect. Rather, assuming a masculine guise affords certain privileges that are key to fully grasping the point of this custom and of how the United States affords opportunities for men that are often not open to women.

Continuing this trend of social critique, teachers can have students analyze the ways that Sam navigates societal structures to hide his sex. Readers can brainstorm a list from the text of the lengths to which Sam goes to avoid revealing his sex. For example, he evades taking off his shirt, "for the same reason he worked on the Bonner's farm. Their school let his work weeding the fields and cutting vines stand in for the PE requirement he'd put off since ninth grade. He couldn't meet it any other way, not if it meant changing for class or team practice in a locker room" (p. 10).

Teachers can ask students why a physical education class would be detrimental to Sam, encouraging students to see how the institution of school is gendered—through sports, locker rooms, and bathrooms, for instance. Students might complete a scavenger hunt (Pennell, 2017) to note the ways their school space is gendered and to relate this to Sam's experiences in the text. For example, beyond gendered locker rooms, many schools have homecoming queens and kings or vote on superlatives for their student bodies, selecting one for each from two genders (i.e., a boy winner and a girl winner).

In addition to these institutional practices, McLemore writes of other personal ways Sam works to avoid his natal sex. She notes, "Sam had practiced driving his pitch lower, so that when other boys, frightened into silence by unexpected cracks and breaks in their own words, emerged with dropped voices, so would he" (p. 81), and Sam binds his breasts and wears loose jeans in order to appear as a boy. They might further explain the references to Sam's appearance and body, explaining how transgender individuals often alter their bodies and noting the ways that society defines gender according to exterior features.

While these practices can have positive effects on a transgender person's emotional and psychological well-being, they can also cause physical harm, such as back pain and even rib fractures from binding (Tsjeng, 2016). Teachers might share this with students to illustrate the severity of the issue. Students could compare Sam's story with those they read in *Beyond Magenta* (Kuklin, 2014), noting how the people about which they read discussed alterations to their appearance and how they might have struggled with recognition.

The notions of sex, gender, and appearance become broader narratives in the novel and ones that teachers can return to as they read. These narratives reflect the discourses often heard in public debates over the rights of transgender individuals. For example, the Bonner sisters threaten to reveal Sam's identity, insisting that Sam is a girl although he does not identify as such. In one instance, Ivy and Miel clash over this topic: Ivy says "she's a girl" (p. 113), to which Miel retorts, "He's not a girl" (p. 114).

During this insistence, the Bonner sister midgenders Sam, referring to him with feminine pronouns, while Miel instead returns to Sam's masculine pronoun, restating *he* in her retort. This battle for pronoun reference is part of a larger misunderstanding that teachers can help rupture through a focus on language and its use. Teachers can remind students that sex and gender are different and can prompt students to identify how pronouns are important and work to identify people.

As part of this lesson on pronouns, teachers might return to the story of the red crayon (Hall, 2015) read prior to the novel and how it might feel to have someone call you something that you truly do not feel you are. Sam later explains how words impact him, thinking:

> The idea of being called Miss or Ms. Or, worse, Mrs. The thought of being grouped in when someone called out *girls* or *ladies*. The endless, echoing use of *she* and *her*, *miss*, and *ma'am*. Yes, these were words, they were all just words. But each of them was wrong, and they stuck to him. Each one was a golden fire ant, and they were biting his arms and his neck and his bound flat chest, leaving him bleeding and burning. (McLemore, 2016, p. 106)

This passage reveals how painful it is for Sam to even think of being labeled wrongly and thus reinforces for students how important it is to ensure that people's identities are respected and correct names and pronouns used.

When Miel insists that Sam is a boy in the exchange above, Ivy, referring to Sam's birth certificate, quips, "That says different" (p. 114). Ivy again reflects a broader discourse that holds that a person's sex assigned at birth should also be one's gender, while Miel disrupts this belief to show that sex and gender are different and to note that if Sam feels authentically a boy, he should be referred to as such. Miel hated Ivy for "her implication that his body made him a girl" (p. 228), illustrating again that one's organs do not define their gender.

In another instance, Miel proclaims, "As though the truth of his body was any of their business, as they had a right to consider how he lived an affront to them" (p. 117). To explore the topics of gender broached here, teachers could ask students: *Who (if anyone) has the right to know a person's sex organs? Why do people feel inclined to ask or know? How are sex and gender related then, if at all?* Teachers might also engage students in the national debate to define gender and sex and the Department of Health and Human Services' efforts "to establish a legal definition of sex under Title IX" (Green, Benner, & Pear, 2018, para. 3). As part of this study, students could investigate primary resources to evaluate the differences between the Obama and Trump administrations' approaches to sex and gender. Teachers could assign students to research different related pieces in small groups and then combine as a class to compare and contrast.

Returning to the novel, as students work to understand Sam's identity and others' reactions, they may also wonder about Miel's relationship with Sam, which was one that was wholly supportive. Readers learn:

> When he was eight, and she walked in on him changing, she didn't scream, or run down the hall. She just shut the door and left, and when he pulled on his jeans and his shirt and went after her, he found her sitting on the back steps. Her expression was so full of wonderment and recognition, as though she almost understood but not quite, that he sat down next to her and told her more than he'd ever planned to. (McLemore, 2016, p. 33)

As the story continues, Miel takes extreme measures to protect Sam and does not question his identity, but rather loves him as a person. McLemore writes, "She understood that with his clothes off, he was the same as he was with them on" (p. 13). Miel thus recognizes that Sam is who he is and that his sex organs do not stand for him entirely. She doesn't ask questions, but silently helps Sam as she can.

We do learn, however, that it is difficult for Miel to know so little about the intricacies of Sam's struggle, and she does in fact have questions. This makes the situation more real and complex; she tells Sam in an intense scene in the novel: "I don't want to push you or confuse you or make you face anything you're not ready for" (p. 139). Her love for him is unconditional, and she puts it before making him explain himself.

Teachers can prompt students to consider the connection between the two protagonists through questions including: *What is the basis of Sam and Miel's relationship? How would you define their bond—is it friendship, romantic love, or something else? How do they support one another? Why doesn't Miel ask more questions? What might she ask if she did? What labels might be ascribed to Miel for loving Sam, and do they fit or not?*

A common response to a situation such as Miel and Sam's is for readers to wonder if Miel is a lesbian if Sam's sex is female. This would be an ideal place to return to conceptions of sexual orientation and gender. While Miel is attracted to Sam as a boy, her total acceptance of him makes her character more dynamic and provides a platform for considering what constitutes relationships and how those stipulations should be only the concern of the individuals involved.

While society might want to place Miel in a box or label her for loving Sam, teachers can remind students that it is always better to allow individuals to self-identify. Teachers could then ask: *How do you think Miel would characterize her sexual orientation? Why—what evidence in the book illustrates that? How would Sam characterize his sexual orientation, and what evidence in the book affords for that classification?*

Beyond the Bonner sisters' rejection and Miel's acceptance of Sam, there are other significant characters whose reactions are important for students to consider to deepen their understandings and empathy toward transgender individuals. Sam's mother is particularly significant, as she allows Sam to live as a boy for her own protection, but she believes he will "grow out of it," as she shares with Miel. During reading, teachers can ask students if they do in fact think Sam will change over the course of the novel. When Sam does tell his mother he wishes to remain as his authentic self, his mother's reaction is perhaps unexpected—without much ado, she accepts Sam's wishes, saying "People should know what they want" (p. 209).

Prior to this scene, students could predict how they think Sam's mother will respond and compose written narratives that imagine the scenario. After the scene in the book, they can compare their own with what actually happens. Students could view videos in which family members of transgender individuals explain their process, such as Kris Jenner on the loss of her husband Bruce (E! Entertainment, 2015), or the parents of Katie Hill and Arin Andrews, two transgender teens who have become famous for their own memoirs (TheAtari400, 2018).

Often, there is a grieving process involved—many describe that they have lost someone in their lives because the person becomes someone different and not the person they feel they knew and loved. Students might also relate the instance in the book in which Sam tells his mother to those "coming out" stories in *Beyond Magenta* (Kuklin, 2014), again to reinforce that not all experiences of trans individuals are the same (Boyd & Bereiter, 2017). In fact, these multiple perspectives would be critical: Sam's mother is much more accepting than many family members, and reading additional narratives would ensure students develop a broad awareness for how difficult this experience can be and would cultivate empathy.

Beyond Sam's gender, other developing storylines in the book also warrant students' attention, especially Miel's background and her fight to piece together her family history. We learn through small glimpses into Miel's memories that her father attempted to rid her of her roses because it was a curse; her mother, rather, tried several different approaches, one of which was to put Miel in a hollowed-out pumpkin.

Teachers can perform close readings of these scenes to determine what happened with Miel's mother in the river and how she and Leandro supposedly died. They might compose imaginary news articles on the ways they perceive the scene and the tragic deaths. Students can explore questions such as: *What did Miel's mom and dad do—how did they handle the roses differently? Whose reaction would you prefer if you were Miel? What could they have done differently? To what extent can we understand their choices?*

Teachers can also lead students through an in-depth analysis of the characters of the Bonner sisters. They could create images of each to separate them according to the qualities demonstrated in specific scenes in the text. They might also consider what stereotypes of women the sisters represent, and they may wish to critique McLemore's presentation (see chapter 7, Women's Rights). The sisters are presented as jealous, immoral, and promiscuous.

While the sisters' actions toward Miel are deplorable, as they blackmail her and lock in her in a coffin, their reputation in the small town in which they live, their parents' confinement of them, and the negative aura around Chloe's pregnancy could be explored for how it represents young women. Students might seek out similar representations of women in contemporary cultures and bring those in for comparison and discussion, leading their classmates through a specific parallel between the book and a current story or event.

After Reading

There are several climactic moments in the text that students can reflect on after reading. For example, Aracely reveals late in the novel that she was Miel's brother and had been waiting for the right time to disclose herself to Miel. Sam had determined earlier who Aracely really was, but he did not share her secret. Students could ponder if this was the right decision on Sam's part and if this subtracted from his relationship with

Miel. Students can also consider, for example: *Was Sam loyal to Miel? Was Miel right to be angry at Aracely for not telling her, given all that Aracely had done to protect and care for her?* Additional climactic moments to analyze are the Bonner sisters' truth-telling episode or the fight between Sam and Miel toward the end of the novel.

Students can also explore how magical elements might both have added to and detracted from the story in its entirety. For example, in Aracely's narrative, considering how she became herself in the water and grew to an older age might both have added to the story (allowing someone to care for Miel) but excluded more detail about how transgender individuals transition. Teachers can ask: *Why would the author represent transgender characters with magical realism—what did this add to the issue, and what might it have left out? What did Miel's roses represent? How did they push the story along, and how did they stall it?* Students might create artistic representations of a magical element of the story and address the metaphors of entities such as the roses, the moon, pumpkins, or the water in their visuals.

At teachers' discretion, students might wish to explore how transgender individuals live their authentic lives. Aracely tells Miel in the novel, "this is me not hiding" (McLemore, 2016, p. 225), and explains what it means for her to live genuinely. Some individuals have surgery, wishing to remove sex organs that feel burdensome and gaining those they feel better reflect their identity. Some take hormones to help them feel more aligned with their gender and to better present that to others, such as through their voice or facial hair, while others do not alter their physical appearance but rather dress as they wish and embody other features such as hair, clothing, and mannerisms that feel authentic to them.

Again, these exist on a spectrum, and helping students see there is not one way to be transgender is crucial. Students might conduct research and share their findings with the class. The Netflix documentary *Growing Up Coy* (Juhola, 2016) or the PBS *Frontline* episode "Growing Up Trans" (Navasky & O'Connor, 2015) could help students understand many of the issues surrounding transgender individuals, including living authentically, family support, and legal policies.

Relatedly, students could research the rights of transgender individuals in the United States and the controversies surrounding those rights. They could investigate local school policies and state ordinances as well as federal legislation. Teachers might assign groups to examine each level or to focus on particular spaces. They might research mandates governing sports at various levels as well, including the Olympics, or they could research specific issues such as bathroom use. They could create multimedia presentations to share the information they learn with their classmates.

IDEAS FOR SOCIAL ACTION

From their research above, students could pinpoint a way they would like to make change to a particular policy or to raise awareness around an issue related to society and gender. If their school does not have gender-inclusive bathrooms, they might wish to lobby their administration for those or they may write to their legislators regarding Bathroom Bills if they are in a state that is considering such legislation. They might wish to make a recommendation to authorities on school sports, dress codes, or even school documents such as identification cards, as many schools unnecessarily require the sex and name assigned at birth on such entities.

Students could also design an awareness campaign simply about pronoun and language use that honors the gender spectrum. Similar campaigns to affirm people's gender and uphold the uniqueness of each individual could be undertaken, with social media postings, videos, and posters made that remind students of the social construction of gender and the need to respect all humans. Especially in reference to the broader narratives that Ivy Bonner insists on, such as referring to Sam as "she" and maintaining that his birth certificate determines his identity, students could work to alter these public discourses.

While Gay-Straight Alliances exist in many schools across the country, such clubs or organizations supporting transgender individuals are less prevalent. Students might wish to create a group that supports the gender spectrum and welcomes individuals who identify along the continuum. They might also take as their mission to disrupt gendered norms in schools in the practices they may have identified earlier in the unit, such as prom king or queen, and offer alternatives that value people as individuals and humans. They might involve faculty in their endeavors, educating their teachers on related gender issues and ways they can de-center gender in their practices or utilize more inclusive practices.

They could also invite guest speakers to their school or classroom who educate others on the gender spectrum as well. Finally, they could establish support networks for transgender students in their school, connecting them with compassionate counselors and teachers and even online resources, as many youths in rural settings often lack the encouragement they need and could benefit from online mentorship.

Students might also wish to research and share famous individuals who are transgender. Telling the stories of others again humanizes the gender spectrum and illustrates that everyone's story who is transgender is not the same. They might choose someone in a realm in which they are interested, such as sports, film, or music, and investigate that person, even potentially interviewing or communicating with them via social media. They could examine songs of transgender musicians such as Namoli Brennet's "Thorn in Your Side" and Skylar Kergil's "Tell Me a Story," for example, and interpret the meanings of the lyrics as well as learn about the artist.

This research could culminate in video compilations that could be shared school and community wide. Bringing to light people who identify as gender variant and helping others see the struggles, successes, and everyday lives of such individuals is necessary. This disruption makes the often unknown and therefore feared more accessible to everyone so that people can begin to understand and affirm.

SUPPLEMENTAL RESOURCES

Canonical Companions

Cyrano de Bergerac by Edmond Rostand
The Count of Monte Cristo by Alexandre Dumas
The Awakening by Kate Chopin
The Scarlet Letter by Nathaniel Hawthorne

Connected Young Adult Literature

Being Emily by Rachel Gold
I am J by Cris Beam
Almost Perfect by Brian Katcher

Beautiful Music for Ugly Children by Kirstin Cronn-Mills

Connected Music

"Thorn in Your Side" by Namoli Brennet
"Tell Me a Story" by Skylar Kergil

REFERENCES

Boyd, A. & Bereiter, T. (2017). "I don't really know what a fair portrayal is and what a stereotype is": Pluralizing transgender narratives with young adult literature. *English Journal, 107*(1), 13–18.

Dale, J. M. (Producer) & del Torro, G. (Director). (2018). *The shape of water* [Motion picture]. Russia: TSG Entertainment.

Davis, H. F. (2017). Why the "transgender" bathroom controversy should make us rethink sex-segregated public bathrooms. *Politics, Groups, and Identities.* doi.org/10.1080/21565503.2017.1338971

Deschamps, J. & Ossard, C. (Producers) & Jeunet, J. (Director). (2001). *Amélie* [Motion picture]. France: UGC-Fox Distribution.

E! Entertainment. (2015, September 27). Kris Jenner breaks down over loss of Bruce [Video file]. Retrieved from https://www.youtube.com/watch?v=l_cfAqnYdhs.

García Márquez, G. (1955). A very old man with enormous wings (Gregory Rabassa, Trans.). Retrieved from https://www.ndsu.edu/pubweb/~cinichol/CreativeWriting/323/Marquez ManwithWings.htm.

García Márquez, G. (1968). The handsomest drowned man in the world (Gregory Rabassa, Trans.). Retrieved from https://www.ndsu.edu/pubweb/~cinichol/CreativeWriting/423/ MarquezHandsomestDrownedMan.htm.

Gay, Lesbian, & Straight Education Network. (2014). Key concepts and terms. Retrieved from https://www.glsen.org/sites/default/files/GLSEN%20Terms%20and%20Concepts%20 Thematic.pdf.

Green, E. L., Benner, K., & Pear, R. (2018). "Transgender" could be defined out of existence under Trump administration. *New York Times.* Retrieved from https://www.nytimes.com/ 2018/10/21/us/politics/transgender-trump-administration-sex-definition.html.

Greytak, E. A., Kosciw, J. G., & Diaz, E. M. (2009). Harsh realities: The experiences of transgender youth in our nation's schools. A report from the Gay, Lesbian, and Straight Network. Retrieved from https://www.glsen.org/sites/default/files/Harsh%20Realities.pdf.

Hall, M. (2015). *Red, a crayon's story.* New York: Greenwillow Books.

Herman, J. L., Flores, A. R., Brown, T. N. T., Wilson, B. D. M., & Conron, K. J. (2017). Age of individuals who identify as transgender in the United States. *The Williams Institute: UCLA School of Law.* Retrieved from https://williamsinstitute.law.ucla.edu/wp-content/uploads/ TransAgeReport.pdf.

Herthel, J. & Jennings, J. (2014). *I am Jazz.* New York: Dial Books.

Hoffman, J. (2016, June 30). Estimate of U.S. transgender population doubles to 1.4. million adults. *New York Times.* Retrieved from https://www.nytimes.com/2016/07/01/health/ transgender-population.html.

Holden, D. (2018, February 12). The Education Department officially says it will reject transgender student bathroom complaints. Buzzfeed News. Retrieved from https://www. buzzfeed.com/dominicholden/edu-dept-trans-studentbathrooms?utm_term=.hvKYV41 MW#.ovbdGBPqz.

Jeffries, M. & Boyd, A. (2018). Cultivating resilience and resistance in Trump's America: Employing critical hope as a framework in LGBTQ+ centers. *Journal of Critical Scholarship on Higher Education and Student Affairs, 3*(3), 26–37.

Juhola, E. (Director). (2016). *Growing up Coy* [Video file]. Retrieved from https://www.netflix.com/title/80128657.

Kralik, J. (2017, July 28). "Bathroom bill" legislative tracking. *National Conference of State Legislatures.* Retrieved from http://www.ncsl.org/research/education/-bathroom-bill-legislative-tracking635951130.aspx.

Kuklin, S. (2014). *Beyond magenta: Transgender teens speak out.* Somerville, MA: Candlewick.

Mattingly, E. (2013). Lesson 1: Magical elements in magical realism. EDSITEment! The best of humanities on the web. Retrieved from https://edsitement.neh.gov/lesson-plan/lesson-1-magical-elements-magical-realism.

McLemore, S. (2016). *When the moon was ours.* New York: Thomas Dunne Books.

Meerwijk, E. L. & Sevelius, J. M. (2017). Transgender population size in the United States: A meta-regression of population-based probability samples. *American Journal of Public Health, 107*(2), 1–8. 10.2105/AJPH.2016.303578

Mythology & Fiction Explained. (2017, December 7). La Llorona: The weeping woman (urban legend explained) [Video file]. Retrieved from https://www.youtube.com/watch?v=35dSLDGI3DM.

Navasky, M. & O'Connor, K. (Directors & Producers). (2015, June 30). Growing up trans [Television series episode]. Retrieved from https://www.pbs.org/wgbh/frontline/film/growing-up-trans/.

Pennell, S. M. (2017). Training secondary teachers to support LGBTQ+ students: Practical applications from theory and research. *High School Journal, 101*(1), 62–72.

Roloff, R. & Boyd, A. (2018). Learning to live authentically: Studying a transgender perspective through *Being Emily.* In P. Greathouse, B. Eisenbach, & J. Kaywell (Eds.), *Queer adolescent literature as a complement to the English language arts curriculum* (pp. 211–220). Lanham, MD: Rowman & Littlefield.

"Terms and Definitions." (2018). Gender Identity/Expression and Sexual Orientation Resource Center. Washington State University. Retrieved from https://thecenter.wsu.edu/education/terms-and-definitions/.

TheAtari400. (2018, April 29). Arin Andrews & Katie Hill—transgender teen couple [ABC *20/20* Full Version] [Video file]. Retrieved from https://www.youtube.com/watch?v=Of6XU5LhRuI.

Tsjeng, Z. (2016, September 28). Inside the landmark, long overdue study on chest binding. *Broadly.* Retrieved from https://broadly.vice.com/en_us/article/7xzpxx/chest-binding-health-project-inside-landmark-overdue-transgender-study.

Weiser, K. (2017). La Llorona—Weeping woman of the Southwest. Retrieved from https://www.legendsofamerica.com/gh-lallorona/.

"Youth and Students." (2018). National Center for Transgender Equality. Retrieved from https://transequality.org/issues/youth-students.

Zanuck, R. D., Cohen, B., & Jinks, D. (Producers) & Burton, T. (Director). (2003). *Big fish* [Motion picture]. United States: Columbia Pictures.

5

HUMAN TRAFFICKING

According to the US Department of Homeland Security, human trafficking is "modern-day slavery and involves the use of force, fraud, or coercion to obtain some type of labor or commercial sex act" (n.d., para. 1). With roots in ancient Greek and medieval times, to slavery, and to sweat shops, countries around the world have a sordid history regarding "the exploitation of vulnerable populations—predominately women and children—for financial gain" (Wilson, 2011, para. 7).

According to a the International Labour Organization, an estimated 40.3 million people are currently in slavery worldwide. Some "81% of these people are trapped in forced labor; 25% of them are children; and 75% are women and girls" (Polaris, 2018, para. 2). While a worldwide issue and often thought of as something that happens only overseas, human trafficking is also pervasive in the United States, with California, Texas, and Florida leading the states in numbers of human trafficking cases (National Human Trafficking Hotline, 2017).

According to a study of human trafficking in the state of Texas, there are currently an estimated 313,000 reported cases of human trafficking, including 79,000 minors involved in sex trafficking incidents (Busch-Armendariz, Nale, Kammer-Kerwick, Kellison, Torres, Cook-Heffron, & Nehme, 2016). In addition to sex trafficking, child labor and forced marriages are two other forms of trafficking that most commonly affect children and young adults worldwide. The Tahirih Justice Center reported three thousand suspected forced marriage cases in the United States between 2009 and 2011 (2018, para. 5), and child labor trafficking is common in a variety of countries due to the demand for cheap labor to profit off a business that is otherwise not as profitable.

Although in 2011 President Obama designated January as Human Trafficking Month in an attempt to raise awareness of this pervasive international issue, many misconceptions about human trafficking abound, such as that human trafficking doesn't happen in the United States, human trafficking is only sex trafficking, and trafficking victims are always either foreigners or people who are poor (US Department of Homeland Security, n.d.).

As such, in order to clear up misperceptions, as well as to inform students about this pervasive human rights issue and to help them identify ways in which to keep themselves and others safe, teachers should consider a unit of study on human trafficking. In this chapter we will use the book *The Queen of Water* as the focal text upon which to support an investigation of human trafficking, both in the United States and abroad.

THE QUEEN OF WATER

The Queen of Water by Laura Resau and María Virginia Farinango (2011) shares the story of coauthor Farinango's childhood. It is a work of fiction based in fact; María Virginia writes that "the bones and blood of the story you have read are true. My imagination has fleshed out the details and shaped it into its final form" (p. 346). This book offers readers a look at the complexity of human trafficking in the modern day.

María Virginia was born in Ecuador, in a poor indigenous Andean village. When she is seven years old, with her parents' permission in the hope that she will have a better life away from their extremely impoverished home, she is taken from her village to be a servant for a mestizo (the ruling class of Spanish descendants) couple.

Though agreements regarding salary and visits home have been arranged, this new family does not follow through. María Virginia must cook, clean, and take care of children for no pay, with the mother of the family beating her when the work is not done to her satisfaction. As the book progresses, the reader follows María Virginia through her childhood to young adulthood as she is raised as a servant, tries to educate herself, comes of age, and eventually comes to terms with her family, her background, her culture, and herself.

While there are multiple texts that can be used for a study on human trafficking (see Connected Young Adult Literature), this book was chosen for a variety of reasons. First, it takes place in Ecuador, and as such offers a global perspective in a setting that most likely will be unfamiliar to many students. Parsons and Rietschlin (2014) posit that, "Many adolescents learn about global issues through mass media or video games that focus on 'catastrophe, terrorism, and war' (Short, 2012, p. 13), resulting in superficial understandings and fear-based perspectives on those who live outside of the United States. However, adolescents may develop deeper connections and understandings through engagement with global young adult (YA) literature" (p. 130).

Books like *The Queen of Water*, based on one girl's childhood and young adult experiences, can offer students perspectives on global issues they may have not previously considered. Moreover, as this book does not revolve around sex trafficking, it can help to combat stereotypes about what all human trafficking encompasses. For example, an examination of María Virginia's family and her conflicted feelings about both them and her culture might help students consider the complexity of human trafficking—why families might be compelled to "sell" their children, why children might be hesitant to seek help to escape their situations, and the personal and psychological implications for families who have firsthand experience with trafficking.

TEACHING STRATEGIES

Before Reading

Before reading this or any other book on modern-day trafficking, teachers will need to provide some background information regarding trafficking around the world today. General statistics, such as those presented above, can prove helpful in introducing students to the prevalence of trafficking.

For example, sharing that according to the FBI, human trafficking is "believed to be the third-largest criminal activity in the world. . . . It involves both U.S. citizens and foreigners alike, and has no demographic restrictions" (n.d., para. 1), as well as providing students with visual images to complement numeric statistics, would likely be helpful. This way, students can see just how many people this social problem actually affects. Students can even create their own visual representations of the information and statistics they find, be it types of trafficking, locations of trafficking, or the history of trafficking around the world.

There are a variety of teaching resources for teachers interested in conducting units of study on human trafficking that will work well as an introduction to this issue. For example, the Frederick Douglass Family Initiative website offers teachers free service learning curriculum for a project called "Globalize 13." Created to celebrate and spread awareness of the Thirteenth Amendment's 150th anniversary in 2015, available materials provide "a study of the various forms of labor trafficking and why slavery still exists in the products we consume every day . . . (and) suggestions on how students, in the spirit of Abraham Lincoln and the 13th Amendment, can take action to end slavery" (Frederick Douglass Family Initiatives Project, 2007–2018, para. 1).

The *New York Times* offers curriculum titled "What Is Modern Slavery? Investigating Human Trafficking" that can be used in conjunction with articles from the newspaper (Oljavo, 2012). While a bit dated, teachers can use these activities as an introduction to modern-day trafficking, and then have students research more current news stories on forced servitude. Using newspapers as examinations of primary source documents, teachers can lead students in scrutinizing news stories for credibility and explicit and implicit biases. Teachers can ask students to identify, based on a chosen new article, what the journalist's stance on the issue is, and how they came to that conclusion (e.g., through the writer's chosen words, accompanying photographs, etc.).

UNICEF (n.d.) also offers an in-depth curriculum on child trafficking. With activities, handouts, role-plays, survivor stories, and suggested resources for both middle school– and high school–aged students, this free curriculum is connected to Common Core Standards and would prove valuable in helping teachers provide an overview of the various aspects of child trafficking around the world today. Students can read survivor stories and then recreate those stories through poetry or art, then compare the narratives across the class to establish similarities and differences.

In all cases, teachers should take care to explicitly address key issues surrounding and intertwined with forcible servitude. According to Dragiewicz (2008), issues of "privilege, power, and oppression"; "attitudes about poverty"; "racism" and "'othering'" of different cultures"; "attitudes about migration"; "attitudes about sex work and sex workers"; "attitudes about gender, sex and sexuality"; "variation within feminism"; "data reliability issues"; "history of trafficking"; and "definitional and terminological debates" (pp. 189–192) are all topics that teachers should consider weaving into a unit of study on human trafficking.

By asking students to consider these issues: *What do you think about sex workers?*; *How might one's (lack of) income contribute to falling into a trafficking situation?*; *Why do you think there might not be accurate information about the scope and prevalence of trafficked humans around the world?*, for example, teachers can help students to see the complexity of trafficking.

Before reading, teachers can give students a preunit opinionaire or anticipation guide, asking them to privately identify their knowledge and beliefs about trafficking. Students can identify to what extent they agree with statements like *Human trafficking mostly takes place in developing countries. The majority of human trafficking situations are related to sex workers. Most people who are trafficked have chosen a lifestyle of drugs and alcohol.*

At the end of the unit, students can revisit their answers and determine if their opinions and knowledge have changed. As it is likely that they will have some changes in opinion, teachers can guide students in reflecting upon where their original opinions came from, and, hopefully, come to the conclusion that all challenging issues are never as simple as they might first seem.

During Reading

Author Laura Resau's official website offers a plethora of resources that are useful for leading during-reading activities. The website also provides interviews of María Virginia, so students can see and hear firsthand accounts from the author/protagonist of the book. In addition to interviews with María Virginia, the website has links to videos, maps, and articles about Ecuador. In viewing these, students can learn about a country and culture for which they may have no previous experience and have a visual of the setting to enhance their reading, understanding, and enjoyment of the book.

Throughout the book, María Virginia mentions her love of MacGyver. Teachers can show clips from the 1980s television show and lead students in contemplating what it is about MacGyver that would be so appealing to María Virginia. They can also brainstorm current television shows that María Virginia might enjoy, creating a "playlist queue" with brief explanations of each of their choices in order to demonstrate their understanding of the book in general, and protagonist María Virginia in particular.

While reading *The Queen of Water*, students can choose one area of trafficking (e.g., sex workers, forced labor, child soldiers) to research. In a jigsaw format, they can share the information they have gathered on their chosen topic with their classmates, making connections to the depictions of trafficking presented in the book. In this way, they can focus on their own interests, but still learn of the various types of trafficking that exist in the world today.

For example, students who are interested in learning more about sex trafficking can make connections to how over time, María Virginia might not have previously considered forced labor as a component of human trafficking. While protagonist María Virginia is sold to a family to work domestically, taking care of the children, cleaning, and cooking, there are also companies, groups, and individuals that use child and forced labor in other ways around the world.

According to the United States Department of Labor, "As of September 30, 2016, the List of Goods Produced by Child Labor or Forced Labor comprises 139 goods from 75 countries" including bananas, bricks, broccoli, carpets, and cashews (n.d., para. 8). In order to better understand the variety of goods and services that may be manufactured by trafficked workers, students can take an interactive quiz on the website slaveryfootprint.com.

Here, students individually submit answers to questions like what kinds of foods they eat, what types of electronics are in their home, the amount of clothes they own, and more. At the end of the survey, individuals are given the "number of slaves working for you," as well as a link for learning more about where to buy and not buy products and how student groups can partner to promote equitable labor and boycott identified companies that use unethical practices (Made in a Free World, 2017). It will be important for teachers to emphasize that this activity is not to instill guilt in students but rather to develop their awareness and therefore ability to act with their new knowledge.

Connected to child labor is the conscription of children under the age of fifteen into the military. The forced use of child soldiers might be a specific topic of interest to students, and they might want to, for example, research how and why children become soldiers as well as the challenges of getting out of this situation. There are many resources available to guide educators in teaching about child soldiers, and the memoir *A Long Way Gone: Memoirs of a Boy Soldier* (Beah, 2007) is a powerful text that can be used to explore the issue of child slavery (Darragh & Boyd, 2018). (See also chapter 6, Refugee Crisis.)

Sex trafficking, while not the focus of the novel *The Queen of Water*, is another facet of human trafficking that students might be interested in researching. With regard to victims of child sex trafficking in the United States, those who run away from home for whatever reason have a greater risk of finding themselves in a trafficking situation.

In 2016, for example, "an estimated 1 out of 6 endangered runaways reported to the National Center for Missing and Exploited Children were likely child sex trafficking victims. Of those, 86% were in the care of social services or foster care when they ran" (Polaris, The facts, 2018, para. 1). Statistics like these shed light on how one might easily fall into a trafficking situation, as well as why it may seem impossible to escape.

Teachers and students can also peruse the National Human Trafficking Hotline website and read "inspiring stories of individuals who have reached out to the National Human Trafficking Hotline for help, and the advocates, agents, and members of the community who have worked tirelessly to ensure that the needs of victims and survivors are met" (Polaris, National human trafficking hotline, 2018, para. 1), or read news stories regarding trafficking on the United States Immigration and Customs Enforcement (ICE) website (n.d.), which has links to current new releases where students can read about up-to-date human smuggling/trafficking cases.

While it is possible that students' knowledge of ICE relates only to immigration and the separation of families, ICE has been in place for a number of years and has been instrumental in raising awareness of human trafficking and providing help for victims. A look into their work can help shed light on a more positive side of trafficking—those who are both supporting the victims and trying to stop the perpetrators.

In addition, students can look at the National Human Trafficking Hotline website to identify how many human trafficking cases were reported by characteristics such as state, gender, age, and type of trafficking. As all states are represented, these statistics might help students to see that this is not something that just happens elsewhere, it may be happening in their own communities as well.

To deepen understanding about how someone might fall into a trafficking situation, the website and app "BALKANS ACT NOW!: Ban human trafficking" (2014) has not only information regarding learning more about and recognizing and reporting trafficking, but also an interactive game. Players choose a character (based on real stories) and walk through a series of scenarios where they must choose how they would respond. At the end of the game, players find out if they escaped the trafficking situation or not.

The game sheds light on the complexity of trafficking—how one small incident or choice can lead to a trafficking scenario, how easily one can become a victim, and how difficult it might be to get free. Students can use this simulation as a springboard to design their own scenarios around María Virginia's story and make predictions about the ending.

A similar game that can be played on the website or via a downloaded app, ACT (Awareness Combats Trafficking), is a "story-based educational game (that) will make you think twice about things you've never even noticed before" (2016, para. 1). Geared specifically toward junior high and high school students, this interactive game helps teens "to identify red flags and warning signs of trafficking" (para. 1). After playing, students might then make a checklist of things to be aware of in their own communities and speculate how these relate to María Virginia's story.

Finally, while reading, students might be interested in comparing modern-day human trafficking with historical accounts of slavery. They can consider, for example, *Who is doing the trafficking?*; *Who is being trafficked?*; *Where is the trafficking taking place?*; *Why is the trafficking happening?*; and *What are the complications regarding getting out of a trafficking situation?* Pairing a slave narrative with a current trafficking story can lead to deeper understanding and richer discussions in and out of class.

After Reading

There are a variety of discussion questions that can help students better understand concepts, themes, and connections in the book. Author Laura Resau's website (2017) offers a link to discussion questions that can help students to make text-to-self-connections and to improve their critical-thinking skills. For example, one posed multipart question is:

> One theme in the novel is the treatment of Ecuador's indigenous habitants. What do María Virginia's interactions with Nino Carlitos, Romelia, Don Walter, and Sonia tell you about attitudes toward indigenous people in Ecuador? What might account for how each of these characters treated María Virginia? What parallels can you draw between treatment of indigenous groups in the U.S. and Ecuador?" (Primary Source, 2017, para. 1)

Questions like these can guide students in thinking about the treatment of indigenous groups in their own communities—at the state, local, and national levels.

Additional inquiries for students are: "Another theme in the novel is involuntary servitude. Why do you think María Virginia's parents agreed to let her go with Nino Carlitos and Romelia? What do you think they expected to happen? How does María Virginia's experience compare to and contrast with other examples of historic and contemporary slavery?" (Primary Source, 2017, para. 1). Thoughtful discussion of these questions can help students to contextualize trafficking from historical and contemporary perspectives, using textual support/examples from the book to further demonstrate their thinking.

Parsons and Rietschlin (2014), in their chapter "The Emigrant, Immigrant, and Trafficked Experiences of Adolescents: Young Adult Literature as Window and Mirror," identify universal themes that can be found in young adult literature portraying the trafficked experience, and teachers can guide students in examining whether the book *The Queen of Water* exemplifies these themes. They write:

> Tangentially reflecting the great ideas and basic psychological needs, the strong universal themes we identified are compassion, education, family, and storytelling. . . . Furthermore, naming was a strong theme. . . . Since the primary objective of the trafficker is to strip the victim of his or her personhood, denying the use of given names is a common dehumanizing technique. Naming is crucial to identify and agency (Trites, 1997), and reclaiming one's name is an act of resistance. (p. 133)

Students can track in what ways these themes are developed through-out the book and brainstorm other examples from literature, history, film, and current events that share similar themes.

After reading the book, teachers might want to guide students in con-ducting further and more in-depth research on one or multiple facets of human trafficking explored in this chapter, as social action projects may arise from students' individual interests. An exploration of how the arts have addressed trafficking could be effective as well.

There are, for example, many songs that address trafficking. Sinead O'Connor's song "This Is to Mother You" was remade by Mary J. Blige and released on the International Day to Abolish Slavery in 2009, with proceeds going to support GEMS: Girls Educational and Mentoring Ser-vices, a Harlem-based agency that provides counseling and support to young victims of sex trafficking. Metal group For Today's song "Fight the Silence" is also about human trafficking, with proceeds from the song and album (also titled *Fight the Silence*) donated to the A21 campaign, a nonprofit organization that "fights human trafficking on a global scale by rescuing and rehabilitating those who have been victimized and helping oppose and prosecute traffickers" (Bowar, 2013, para. 5).

Students can consider songwriters' choice of lyrics, instrumentation, and tone when composing about a specific cause and identify other songs that intentionally or unintentionally depict the trafficking experience. Teachers can also lead students in comparing songs about past and mod-ern slavery—listening to songs of freedom, survival, the Underground Railroad, and traditional spirituals and contrasting the lyrics, themes, and tones with more current songs about human trafficking, using a Venn diagram or other concept map in order to categorize their findings. The identified similarities and differences can be used as a springboard to discuss how the enslavement of humans has (and has not) changed over the years.

With regard to visual literacy, there are numerous documentaries about human trafficking that can offer a richer picture of what trafficking is, what it can look like, and whom it can affect. Care must always be taken in choosing films in the classroom, and with this sensitive topic, teachers will want to be especially judicious. The documentary *Not My Life* (Bilheimer, 2011) is recommended by UNICEF as an appropriate film to introduce students to the trafficking of children around the world, including the United States. The film has a companion website that offers resources including a discussion guide, viewing guide, articles, and websites that can assist educators who want to use it with young people (Worldwide Documentaries, 2018).

While the documentary *I Am Jane Doe* (Mazzio & Sokolow, 2017) has more explicit material, it is a powerful look at the use of social media and the internet as vehicles to traffic humans, specifically young girls, for sex. This film is important for both teens and caretakers alike as it shows how easily young girls and boys can be targeted, taken, and exploited as well as the legal issues surrounding using the internet in this way. Teachers might want to lead a schoolwide event, partnering with counselors, community health specialists, and local police to have a viewing and discussion of the film.

There are a multitude of government and nonprofit groups worldwide that try to combat human trafficking, raise awareness, and provide support for those who have been trafficked. The Blue Campaign, for example, "is the unified voice for the U.S. Department of Homeland Security's (DHS) efforts to combat human trafficking. Working in collaboration with law enforcement, government, non-governmental and private organizations, the Blue Campaign strives to protect the basic right of freedom and to bring those who exploit human lives to justice" (US Department of Homeland Security, n.d., para. 1).

There are also numerous nonprofits that "lead the fight against human trafficking" (Stevens-Kittner, 2017), such as Hagar, Liberty Asia, A21, and Polaris, that students can research in order to gain not only knowledge but also ideas for social action projects in their schools and communities. Students might want to choose one such group to research, preparing a poster or paper of their findings and practicing their formatting skills.

IDEAS FOR SOCIAL ACTION

There are a multitude of social action projects that students can consider, and, of course, in all cases, they should be encouraged to develop their own projects inspired by the topic, their own research, and/or the text they read. In helping students to identify social action projects, teachers might find the website https://issuu.com/alliemerrick/docs/sex_trafficking_02 a useful resource (Merrick, 2014).

This website offers a "sex trafficking social action toolkit" that provides information on policies and legislation connected to sex trafficking; US program resources; links to articles, videos, and electronic resources; and ideas to "Take Action" organized in time commitments (one minute to one hour, to ongoing). These social action suggestions, such as "join an anti-human/sex trafficking organization, spread the word through art, and host a party screening of a movie about anti-human/sex trafficking (Merrick, 2014) might inspire students to either select their own project from the list or to create a new one.

Students might want to raise awareness about human trafficking by researching statistics, warning signs, and where to get help and/or to report suspected trafficking. Specifically, students can create an information/awareness campaign in their school and/or community. They can research some of the key indictors (e.g., stopped attending school, has bruises in various stages of healing, appears to be coached on what to say) that someone is being trafficked, as well as information about how to report suspected trafficking situations and where to get help. These fliers could be posted via social media and/or in locations where teens generally spend their time, both in schools and/or throughout the community (US Department of Homeland Security).

Other students might be compelled to volunteer for an organization that supports those who help people escape trafficking situations and/or to collect supplies to donate to organizations that assist those who have been trafficked, like toiletries, backpacks, blankets, cell phones, and more. Students might also be compelled to raise money to donate to an antitrafficking nonprofit organization. In order to raise funds, students might, for example, offer their own physical labor (e.g., mowing lawns, cleaning a community park) in exchange for donations to support anti–child labor and forced labor organizations.

Likewise, they could use donated money to support organizations like Sanctuary Spring (2012), which employs survivors of trafficking in creating greeting cards, or the Not for Sale Campaign (2016), which supports antitrafficking projects around the world. Students can, for example, purchase some of the greeting cards from Sanctuary Spring and then send them to people in their community who might need some support, like those in the hospital or a nursing home.

Or they could purchase T-shirts and promote the products identified on the Not for Sale website, designing a raffle for them and learning the power of being an informed consumer and the choices they have in where to spend their money and whom to fund.

Students who are interested in child and forced labor in the business sector might be interested in researching companies that have strict policies against child labor and unfair labor practices and spread the word to support those businesses. Similarly, they might want to research companies and products that are known to use and may be more likely to use child labor or practice unethical servitude and raise awareness and speak out against those companies and/or products.

They can encourage local businesses to "take steps to investigate and prevent human trafficking in their supply chains and publish the information, including supplier or factory lists, for consumer awareness" (US Department of State, n.d., para 3) through letters, face-to-face discussions, or writing a letter to the editor of a local newspaper.

Human trafficking is a topic that is scary, sad, and often unspeakable. However, trafficking abounds, in various formats, throughout the world today, and it is only through awareness of this issue and concerted efforts to combat it that its prevalence will be diminished. Lookadoo (2017) writes, "When one considers the fact that abolitionists of the past stood up against and successfully ended slavery when it was legal in this country; imagine the possibilities when today's youth are equipped and empowered to end modern slavery in a world where slavery is illegal in every country" (para. 15). In choosing to courageously take on the difficult topic of human trafficking, teachers can lead the battle, arming their students with knowledge and skills to develop action projects that will inspire current and future service as modern-day abolitionists.

SUPPLEMENTAL RESOURCES

Canonical Companions

Narrative of the Life of Frederick Douglass by Frederick Douglass
Beloved by Toni Morrison
Adventures of Huckleberry Finn by Mark Twain

Connected Young Adult Literature

The Astonishing Life of Octavian Nothing, Traitor to the Nation by M.
   T. Anderson
A Long Way Gone: Memoirs of a Boy Soldier by Ishmael Beah
Copper Sun by Sharon Draper
Hidden Girl: The True Story of a Modern-Day Child Slave by Shyima
   Hall
Tricks by Ellen Hopkins
Sold by Patricia McCormick

Connected Music

"Blood into Gold" by Peter Buffett and Akon
"Fight the Silence" by For Today
"Queen of the Field" by Alicia Keyes
"Redemption Song" by Bob Marley
"This Is to Mother You" by Sinead O'Connor

REFERENCES

A21. (2018). We are the new abolitionists. Retrieved from http://www.a21.org/content/who-we-are/gnihwo.
ACT!: Awareness Combats Trafficking. (2016). Learn to identify the signs. Retrieved from http://www.lifeboat-act.com/#about.
BALKANS ACT NOW!: Ban human trafficking. (2014). Retrieved from http://banhumantrafficking.com/en/home.
Beah, I. (2007). *A long way gone: Memoirs of a boy soldier.* New York: Sarah Crichton Books.
Bilheimer, R. (Director). (2011). *Not my life.* [Motion picture]. United States: Worldwide Documentaries.
Bowar, C. (2013). For Today's video for "Fight the Silence" raises awareness about human trafficking. Retrieved from http://loudwire.com/for-today-video-fight-the-silence-raises-awareness-human-trafficking/.
Busch-Armendariz, N. B., Nale, N. L., Kammer-Kerwick, M., Kellison, B., Torres, M. I. M., Cook-Heffron, L., & Nehme, J. (2016). Human trafficking by the numbers: Initial benchmarks of prevalence & economic impact in Texas. Austin, TX: Institute on Domestic Violence & Sexual Assault, The University of Texas at Austin.
Darragh, J. J. & Boyd, A. S. (2018). We were dangerous and brainwashed to kill: Death and resilience in *A Long Way Gone: Memoirs of a Boy Soldier.* In M. Falter & S. Bickmore (Eds.), *Moving beyond personal loss to societal grieving* (pp. 113–124). Lanham, MD: Rowman & Littlefield.
Dragiewicz, M. (2008). Teaching about trafficking: Opportunities and challenges for critical engagement. *The Feminist Teacher, 18*(3), 185–201. Retrieved from http://traffickinggroundtable.org/wp-content/uploads/2012/11/DRAGIEWICZ-2008-Teaching-about-Trafficking-Opportunities-and-Chal.pdf.

FBI. (n.d.). Human trafficking/involuntary servitude. Retrieved from https://www.fbi.gov/investigate/civil-rights/human-trafficking.

Frederick Douglass Family Initiatives Project. (2007–2018). Welcome to globalize 13. Retrieved from http://www.globalize13.org/sign_up.

Lookadoo, R. (2017, July 27). Human trafficking and teacher awareness: Equipping teachers with knowledge and resources to combat human trafficking. Retrieved from https://www.campbellsville.edu/blog/human-trafficking-teacher-awareness-equiping-teachers-knowledge-resources-combat-human-trafficking/.

Made in a Free World. (2017). How many slaves work for you? Retrieved from https://slaveryfootprint.org.

Mazzio, M. & Sokolow, A. (Producers), & Mazzio, M. (Director). (2017). *I am Jane Doe.* [Motion picture]. United States: 50 Eggs, Inc.

Merrick, A. (2014, October 13). Sex trafficking social action toolkit: From inspiration to action—social action toolkits produced with purpose [Video file]. Retrieved from https://issuu.com/alliemerrick/docs/sex_trafficking_02.

National Human Trafficking Hotline. (2017). National human trafficking hotline data report. Retrieved from https://humantraffickinghotline.org/sites/default/files/2016%20National%20Report.pdf.

Not for Sale. (2016). Not for sale campaign. Retrieved from https://www.notforsalecampaign.org/our-process/.

Ojalvo, H. E. (2012). What is modern slavery? Investigating human trafficking. Retrieved from https://learning.blogs.nytimes.com/2012/03/06/what-is-modern-slavery-investigating-human-trafficking/?_r=0.

Parsons, L. T. & Rietschlin, A. (2014). The emigrant, immigrant, and trafficked experiences of adolescents: Young adult literature as window and mirror. In C. Hill (Ed.), *The critical merits of young adult literature* (pp. 130–156). New York: Routledge.

Polaris. (2018). The facts. Retrieved from https://polarisproject.org/human-trafficking/facts.

Polaris. (n.d.). National human trafficking hotline. Retrieved from https://humantraffickinghotline.org/type-trafficking/human-trafficking.

Primary Source. (2017). *The queen of water* discussion questions and vocabulary. Retrieved from http://resources.primarysource.org/c.php?g=768031&p=5508523.

Resau, L. (2017). *The queen of water* readers' guide. Retrieved from https://www.lauraresau.com/the-queen-of-water-readers-guide.

Resau, L. & Farinango, M. V. (2011). *The queen of water.* New York: Ember.

Sanctuary Spring. (2012). Changing lives in the Philippines one card at a time. Retrieved from http://www.sanctuaryspring.com/index.php.

Stevens-Kittner, N. (2017, July 28). 7 non-profits leading the fight against human trafficking. *Salesforce.* Retrieved from https://www.salesforce.org/7-nonprofits-leading-fight-human-trafficking/.

Tahirih Justice Center. (2018). Works cited. Retrieved from https://www.tahirih.org/works-cited/.

UNICEF. (n.d.). Child trafficking. Retrieved from https://www.unicefusa.org/sites/default/files/6-8_Child_Trafficking_MS_2016.pdf.

United States Department of Homeland Security. (n.d.). Blue campaign: One voice. One mission. End human trafficking. Retrieved from https://www.dhs.gov/blue-campaign/about-blue-campaign.

United States Department of Labor. (n.d.). List of goods produced by child labor or forced labor. Retrieved from https://www.dol.gov/agencies/ilab/reports/child-labor/list-of-goods?page=5.

United States Department of State. (n.d.). 5 ways you can help fight human trafficking. Retrieved from https://www.state.gov/j/tip/id/help/.

United States Immigration and Customs Enforcement (ICE). (n.d.) Retrieved from https://www.ice.gov/news/all.

University of Texas. (2016). Human trafficking by the numbers. Retrieved from https://www.scribd.com/document/337465150/Human-Trafficking-by-the-Numbers-2016#from_embed.

Wilson, D. M. (2011). Human trafficking: Slavery never went away, and students need to know how it affects today's world. *Teaching Tolerance, 39.* Retrieved from https://www.tolerance.org/magazine/spring-2011/human-trafficking.

Worldwide Documentaries. (2018). *Not my life*: A film about slavery in our time. Retrieved from https://www.notmylife.org.

6

REFUGEE CRISIS

One in every 113 people, totaling over 65 million people worldwide, are currently refugees, internally displaced persons, or asylum seekers. This constitutes the largest refugee crisis since World War II (Office of the High Commissioner Human Rights, 2018; UNHCR Figures, 2018). With wars, conflicts, and natural and human-made disasters occurring daily, the topic of refugees has been in the past, and most likely will remain, a relevant topic and global issue of high concern.

It is important to understand the distinction among the terms *refugee, internally displaced persons, migrants, immigrants,* and *asylum seekers,* as these words are often (incorrectly) used interchangeably. According to the Department of Homeland Security, a refugee is "a person outside his or her country of nationality who is unable or unwilling to return to his or her country of nationality because of persecution or a well-founded fear of persecution on account of race, religion, nationality, membership in a particular social group, or political opinion" (Department of Homeland Security, 2018, para. 1).

This contrasts with internally displaced person (IDP), or an individual who is "forcibly uprooted within his or her country but who has not crossed an international border" (Office of the High Commissioner Human Rights, 2018, para. 5). IDPs remain in their own countries but are forced to leave their homes "as a result of armed conflict, human rights violations, or natural or human-made disasters" (para. 1). IDPs and refugees differ from im/migrants, as the latter move to a different country for various reasons but "do not face a direct threat of persecution or death in their home country" (Brown, n.d., Key terms, para. 2).

Finally, an asylum seeker is "a person who has moved across international borders in search of protection and has filed a claim for asylum with the host country's government. While the government reviews the claim, the person remains an asylum seeker. If the claim is accepted, the person becomes a 'refugee' in the eyes of the government" (Brown, Key terms, n.d., para. 6). This chapter will focus on and use the term *refugee*; however, many of the stories told and resources mentioned include people who are asylum seekers and/or the parts of their lives that occurred while they were seeking asylum.

Due to the lack of safety that forces refugees to flee their homes, refugee stories have unique characteristics when compared to stories of immigrants. For example, it is not surprising that the number of refugees in a country correlates with war and political unrest, nor is it startling that refugees have often experienced or witnessed violence and emotional trauma. In fact, reports indicate that "half of refugees are experiencing psychological distress and mental illness resulting from trauma [and that] one fifth of refugee children are also suffering from PTSD" (Finnerty, 2015, paras. 14–15).

While it may be uncomfortable to read some parts of refugee stories, it is important to know the realities this group often experiences in order to better understand the complexities and controversies surrounding this issue. Throughout history, the topic of refugees and other countries' and individual's responsibilities and capacities to provide safe harbor for those in need has been met with controversy, and lack of and/or mis/information has resulted in some people being fearful, unsupportive, or apathetic toward the plight of refugees across the world.

In this chapter, we focus on the refugee crises of the past and present, offering information and resources for teachers to help guide students to better understand what it means to be a refugee, how refugees differ from immigrants, and the policies that impact refugees in the United States and beyond. Of course, in all cases, care and sensitivity must be taken when including literature about refugees into the classroom. A study centered on refugees will most likely include stories of violence, fear, and death. Students, especially those who are refugees, may have experienced trauma and not be ready to participate in class discussions and activities that might trigger painful memories.

THE GIRL FROM ALEPPO:
NUJEEN'S ESCAPE FROM WAR TO FREEDOM

> I hate the word refugee more than any word in the English language. . . . What it really means is a second-class citizen with a number scrawled on your hand or printed on a wristband, who everyone wishes would somehow go away. The year 2015 was when I became a fact, a statistic, a number. Much as I like facts, we are not numbers, we are human beings and we all have stories. This is mine. (Mustafa, 2017, p. 12)

Girl from Aleppo: Nujeen's Escape from War to Freedom (Mustafa, 2017) is the true story of Nujeen Mustafa, a teen with cerebral palsy who journeyed from Syria to Germany in her wheelchair in order to find sanctuary. The book begins with Nujeen's earliest memories of living in Syria.

Born with cerebral palsy, she was unable to go to school, as getting to and from her fifth-floor apartment was nearly impossible. Instead, Nujeen spent her days reading, watching television, and sitting out on the balcony. As the book progresses, the reader learns some history of the conflicts in Syria that ultimately led to Nujeen and her sister's two-month, over-three-thousand-mile journey from Syria to Turkey to Greece to Macedonia to Serbia to Slovenia to Austria to Germany.

Nujeen's first-person teenage explanations of past Syrian rulers and the conflicts connected with them provide an accessible background for students to better understand the long and complicated history of conflict in this country. For example, she describes Assad's father, Hafez, the man "who started the whole family ruling enterprise back in 1970 . . . they ran our country as a police state with fifteen different intelligence agencies, and if people protested they were locked up or killed" (p. 29), and she continues with a brief history of rulers leading to the regime in place at the time the book was written.

Nujeen explains major historical events, like the Damascus Spring, when Bashar became ruler and "released hundreds of political prisoners, allowed intellectuals to have political meetings and authorized the launch of the first independent newspaper. . . . (And also) reduced the retirement age in the army to get rid of his father's old guard" (p. 30), and Bloody Friday, "a black day in the history of Kurds when in 1988, in the final days of the Iran-Iraq War, around twenty of Saddam Hussein's fighter jets swooped down and dropped a deadly mixture of mustard gas and nerve agents on Kurds in the city of Halabja in northern Iraq . . . (and) . . . Thousands of men, women and children were killed . . . . perhaps 5,000, and thousands more were left with their skin all melted and with difficulties breathing" (p. 35). These descriptions help clarify why the family made the decision to have Nujeen and her sister leave home in search of sanctuary.

Traveling by plane, taxi, bus, boat, car, ferry, on foot, and with her sister pushing her in her wheelchair, readers can vicariously experience what it is like for refugees seeking asylum, and, consider, as Nujeen requests later in a TEDx talk, the following points: "First, I am not a number. I am a human. Second, I did not come here because I wanted to, but because I had to. Thirdly, different is not dangerous. And fourth, and most importantly, we (refugees) need your compassion as much as we need your shelter" (TEDx Talk, 2017).

The book concludes with a postscript dated January 2017 explaining that Nujeen had just received asylum/German residency and was going to school with hopes of studying physics in college and becoming an astronaut. Including maps, timelines, and photographs, this book, written from the first-person perspective of a teen who lived a refugee's journey, was chosen because it sheds light on the refugee experience in ways that are accessible to teen readers and that can inspire further investigation into the topics of both refugees and disability, as well as encourage students to consider and share their own personal narratives that might relate.

TEACHING STRATEGIES

Before Reading

Before reading the book, teachers will need to provide some background information regarding what it means to be a refugee as well as past and current refugee crises. There are multiple videos on YouTube that succinctly provide such overviews (e.g., AJ+, 2015; vlogbrothers, 2015). There are also multiple websites from sources like Oxfam, Bridging Refugee Youth and Children's Services, and the BBC that offer curricular resources that could be helpful to teachers who are introducing the topic of refugees to the class.

For example, Brown University's The Choices Program offers on their website a unit of study guiding students to explore geography, data, and personal stories to "consider challenges facing the international community and weigh responses to the crisis" (Refugee Stories, n.d., para. 1). With handouts of key terms, data, maps, and refugee stories as well as video links and a slideshow of maps, this website provides multiple lesson ideas for teachers to help guide students in learning about refugees.

For example, teachers can share maps and videos with students to give them a better understanding of locations that serve as backdrops for the refugee experience. Videos can also provide a visual for students to have a clearer image of the setting of the book. Offering some data and context before reading will help students to better understand and experience Nujeen's story.

Similarly, the United Nations High Commissioner for Refugees (UNHCR) has a website of teaching resources as well a "teaching toolkit" offered in a variety of languages, so teachers can provide materials in a student's primary language if needed (UNHCR Teaching, 2018). The site provides lesson plan ideas, interactive awareness games, and videos. With ready-made discussion questions connected to the videos geared toward specific grade levels, teachers can either choose from those provided or assign different students to watch and respond to different videos. Then in small groups or as a whole class, they can discuss what they learned and identify commonalities in the stories presented.

In addition, the Annenberg Foundation separates the resources regarding learning about refugees on their site into those for teachers and those for students, so teachers can educate themselves before creating lessons for their students. Photos, maps, statistics, and exhibits are some of the many resources provided on this site, and teachers can use the provided teacher resources in order to better prepare themselves to lead discussions and activities on the refugee experience. While a quick search can yield many teaching resources and supports on the topic of refugees, articles by the authors (Darragh, 2017a; Darragh, 2017b; Darragh & Boyd, 2018) might also be helpful in providing some time-saving specific suggestions.

As further introduction to the topic, teachers might encourage students to look at past refugee crises around the world in order to make comparisons to the current situation regarding refugees. Considering World War II, for example, students might investigate the kindertransports of 1938 to

1940, in which nine thousand to ten thousand Jewish children were brought to Great Britain from Nazi Germany (USHMM, n.d.).

Similarly, students might be unfamiliar with Operation Pedro Pan, "a time from December 1960 to October 1962, (when) more than fourteen thousand Cuban youths arrived alone in the United States" (Operation Pedro Pan Group, 2009, para. 2) to escape the Cuban government, which is the "largest recorded exodus of unaccompanied minors in the Western Hemisphere" (para. 2). Unfortunately, there are a multitude of refugee crises students can explore, from Cambodia and Rwanda to the Sudanese Civil War. Students can choose a conflict to research, create a multimedia presentation or a poster to share the information gained with classmates, and then, as a whole class, create a graphic organizer that compares previous conflicts to current ones.

Specific to the Syrian conflict, and with regard to world history and politics, students might consider researching key figures and events referenced in Nujeen's memoir, like the Damascus Spring, Bloody Friday, the Arab Spring, and Assad. As mentioned above, students can create a visual or prepare a short presentation in order to share the information with classmates, and then the class can put all of the information together to create a wiki, a timeline, or a newspaper of events.

During Reading

When teaching about refugees, teachers must be judicious in not using "othering" language, instead focusing on individuals and their humanity. Books like *The Girl from Aleppo* provide an opportunity for students to make text-to-self-connections and realize that refugees are just individuals who have been forced, through no actions of their own, to leave their homes and lives behind in order to be safe. Class discussions should not center solely on the horrors of the situation but on the strength and resilience of the people who are forced to endure such painful struggles as well as the complexity of the refugee crisis.

Discussion questions might center on Nujeen's relationship with members of her family and what her everyday life is like in Syria. *How does Nujeen spend her time? What does she like to do? How does this compare to how you like to spend your time?* Teachers can also lead students in thinking about various journeys they have taken, even if it is a metaphorical journey or a short trip to a neighbor's house.

What has been the most impactful journey you have taken? What were the characteristics of that journey? How did you feel? What obstacles did you face? Was the journey ultimately a success? In helping students to make text-to-self-connections, they can begin to see that, while perhaps they have not had the experience of a refugee, they share the human experience in general and the teen experience in particular with others around the world.

In chapter 8, Nujeen mentions two songs she "discovered" before music was banned in her town: Rodrigo's "Concierto de Aranjuez" and Andrea Bocelli's "Time to Say Goodbye." Teachers can share this music with students, and lead them in contemplating, using textual support, why they think Nujeen enjoyed these particular pieces so much. Students can then create a playlist for Nujeen of other songs they think she might like, or songs that they feel are connected to Nujeen's experiences, indicating at what points in the book the song would be played.

Throughout the book, Nujeen mentions her favorite sayings, such as "Laugh as long as you breathe, love as long as you live" (p. 31), and her life rules, which she calls "Nujeen principles" (p. 31), such as, "I don't believe anyone is born evil, even Assad" (p. 31). Students might track Nujeen's sayings and principles throughout the book and develop their own list of sayings and principles. Students can also track Nujeen's journey on a map, and then write their own literal or metaphorical journey narratives while reading the text.

After Reading

A powerful post-reading activity would be for students to both see and hear Nujeen tell her story after they finish reading her book, and fortunately, there are many interviews with Nujeen available (e.g., O'Connor, 2015). In addition, the *Last Week Tonight with John Oliver* segment that is mentioned in the book is available on YouTube (*Last Week Tonight*, 2015), and Nujeen's TEDx talk "I Am Not a Number: A Refugee's Tale" (TEDx, 2017) is also inspiring and thought-provoking.

Students can also research organizations that provide assistance to refugees, both in the United States and abroad. While it is important to look globally at the refugee crisis, students should consider national and local implications as well. According to the US Department of State (2016), in the fiscal year 2016, communities in the United States welcomed 84,995 refugees from seventy-nine countries, and women and children comprised over 70 percent of the resettled refugees. While California, Texas, New York, Michigan, and Ohio resettled the most refugees, all states have helped and continue to do so (US Department of State, 2016).

Websites like UNHCR (UNHCR Resettlement, 2018) and Office of Refugee Resettlement offer links to local refugee support organizations, and students can find where offices are in their region, state, and local communities. Introducing students to state websites and having them search state and local news sources can illuminate that this is a pervasive issue that spans the continents and inspire them to seek ways to help.

Finally, other books, articles, and films can offer students opportunities to compare and analyze different refugee narratives and formats. Documentaries like *God Grew Tired of Us* (Quinn & Walker, 2006; based on author John Bul Dau's journey to the United States and referenced in the YA book *Lost Boy, Lost Girl: Escaping Civil War in Sudan*) and *Into the Arms of Strangers* (Harris, 2000), about the kindertransports of World War II, are two award-winning films (there are some graphic visuals in each) that offer powerful learning opportunities. In addition, major box office films like *The Good Lie* (Schwartz & Falardeau, 2014) and *First They Killed My Father* (Jolie, Panh, Sarandos, & Viera, 2017) can provide visual learning opportunities for students to consider.

After viewing the film(s), students can make connections to Nujeen's memoir, identifying some similarities among the refugee experiences portrayed. Teachers might also lead students in creating a KWL chart prior to viewing a film, leading students to indicate what they already know and still want to know about the refugee experience. After watching the film(s), students can add to the chart what they have learned and any additional questions they now have. This chart can be hung in the classroom and used as inspiration for ongoing short research searches, papers, and projects, with students filling in the chart when information is gained.

IDEAS FOR SOCIAL ACTION

The message that it is our social responsibility to stand up for, speak out for, and support refugees—one of the most vulnerable populations in the world—is a crucial one for young adults to consider. Teens should be encouraged to develop their own research and social action projects that are connected to the topic of refugees and inspired by the text.

For example, Nujeen laments that in history, we seem to only remember the "bad guys" (p. 175). Students can research people and/or events that made a positive impact in their town, community, and/or state. They can brainstorm ways in which to share this information of positive role models/mentors/events to inspire people to look toward the good in others. For example, students can create posters to hang up in the school or in the community, or they can design a children's picture book to share with elementary school children and have available at their school and local libraries.

As she shares the frustration and confusion in trying to get accurate information while fleeing one's country, Nujeen mentions Bourak, a man from Aleppo who "designed an app called BureauCrazy to help asylum seekers navigate the application process and make the forms available in multiple languages" (p. 260). While that app is currently unavailable, students can design their own app that might help refugees and displaced persons, researching what supports and resources might be needed and what that might look like visually on an app.

In looking at their own communities, students can also research statistics regarding how many refugees are in their own town, state, and/or region. If there are refugee resettlement organizations in their community, they might want to set up an appointment to interview employees and/or volunteers to see what needs the organizations have and identify potential ways in which to help. Students can take the information they learn into their own schools as well. For example, Nujeen mentions how in her school in Germany, "people started a campaign, *Keine Angst* or Don't Be Afraid of Refugees" (p. 276). Students might consider what a similar campaign would look like in their own school and implement one.

Aside from the topic of refugees, students might be inspired by Nujeen's memoir to research topics related to services for people with disabilities, including the history of education for people with disabilities in the United States and the passing of Public Law 94-142, Americans with Disabilities Act. Students can research the current situation regarding education and supports for people with disabilities in other countries as well. Nujeen explains, "In my country there are almost no facilities for disabled people, and the asthma attacks happened so often that I couldn't go to school" (p. 28).

This topic might inspire students to identify resources and barriers for people with disabilities in their own communities. An action project could be, for example, creating a booklet with community resources for refugees, including resources for people with disabilities. The booklet could be available at refugee resettlement centers as well as at schools and health centers for people who work with refugees. Students can research ways in which to make the booklet more accessible to people who may have limited English, such as including visuals, using precise language, and/or having it available in different languages.

Moreover, students can research the accessibility options for buildings in their communities, including their school, and provide recommendations for making spaces and places more accessible for those with mobility challenges. Recommendations could be written as a proposal or in a PowerPoint or other digital presentation format, and perhaps even proposed at a city council or school board meeting if appropriate.

While we have little power to stop the conflicts and disasters that force people to become refugees, we can help students to consider the complexity of the issue and, through reading, to feel just a bit of what it might be like to have to make the impossible decision to leave one's home and life behind in search of safety. We can offer students opportunities to learn more about past refugee crises and compare those to current ones, and we can guide them in creating their own social justice projects that will allow them to speak out for and support refugees, one of the most vulnerable populations in the world.

SUPPLEMENTAL RESOURCES

Canonical Companions

The Odyssey by Homer
Kite Runner by Khaled Hosseini
The Aeneid by Virgil

Connected Young Adult Memoirs

A Long Way Gone: Memoirs of a Boy Soldier by Ishmael Beah

Lost Boy, Lost Girl: Escaping Civil War in Sudan by John Bul Dau and Martha Arual Akech

Taking Flight: From War Orphan to Star Ballerina by Michaela DePrince

I Am Malala: How One Girl Stood Up for Education and Changed the World (Young Readers Edition) by Malala Yousafzai and Patricia McCormick

Connected Young Adult Fiction

I Lived on Butterfly Hill by Marjorie Agosin
Home of the Brave by Katherine Applegate
The Red Umbrella by Christina Gonzalez
Refugee by Alan Gratz
Escape from Aleppo by N. H. Senzai

Connected Music

"Time to Say Goodbye" by Andrea Bocelli
"Wavin' Flag" by K'NAAN
"Safarna Ala Europa" by Ndal Kram
"Blackbird" by The Orchestra of Syrian Musicians
"Concierto de Aranjuez" by Rodrigo

REFERENCES

AJ+. (2015, 8 September). Refugees versus migrants: What's the difference? Retrieved from https://www.youtube.com/watch?v=NethRULYorA.

Annenberg Learner. (2016). In the news: Curriculum resources for teaching about refugees. Retrieved from https://www.learner.org/resources/refugees.

BBC News Services. (2016). Syrian journey: Choose your own escape route. Retrieved from http://www.bbc.com/news/world-middle-east-32057601.

Bishop, R. (1990). Mirrors, windows, and sliding glass doors. *Perspectives, 6* (3), ix–xi.

Bridging Youth and Children's Services. (2017). Immigrant/refugee awareness instructional materials. Retrieved from http://brycs.org/clearinghouse/Highlighted-Resources-Immigrant-Refugee-Awareness-Instructional-Materials.cfm.

Brown University. The choices program. (n.d.). Key terms. Retrieved from https://www.choices.edu/wp-content/uploads/2016/09/choices-twtn-refugee-KeyTerms2017.pdf.

Brown University. The choices program. (n.d.). Refugee stories: Mapping a crisis. Retrieved from https://www.choices.edu/wp-content/uploads/2016/09/choices-twtn-refugee-Mapping Crisis2017.pdf.

Darragh, J. J. (2017a). "Let me help you find your way home": Including the refugee experience in the English language classroom. *WAESOL Educator, 1*(1), 26–30.

Darragh, J. J. (2017b). "Let us pick up our books": Young adult literature and the refugee experience. *The ALAN Review, 44*(3), 13–24.

Darragh, J. J., & Boyd, A. (2018). "We were dangerous, and brainwashed to kill": Death and resilience in *A Long Way Gone: Memoirs of a Boy Soldier.* In M. Falter & S. Bickmore (Eds.), *Moving beyond personal loss to societal grieving: Discussing death's social impact through literature in the secondary ELA classroom*, pp. 137–148. Lanham, MD: Rowman & Littlefield.

Department of Homeland Security. (2018 April 30). Refugees and asylees. Retrieved from https://www.dhs.gov/immigration-statistics/refugees-asylees.

Finnerty, D. (2015). Migrant crisis: Trauma takes toll on mental health. *BBC News*. Retrieved from http://www.bbc.com/news/world-europe-35102320.

Harris, M. J. (Director). (2000). *Into the arms of strangers*. [Motion picture]. United States: Warner Brothers Studio.

Internal Displacement Monitoring Center. (2017). Global report on internal displacement. Retrieved from http://www.internal-displacement.org/global-report/grid2017/.

Jolie, A., Panh, R., Sarandos, T., & Vieira, M. (Producers), & Jolie, A. (Director). (2017). *First they killed my father*. [Motion picture]. United States: Jolie Pas.

Last Week Tonight. (28 September, 2015). Migrants and refugees: *Last week tonight* with John Oliver (HBO). Retrieved from https://www.youtube.com/watch?v=umqvYhb3wf4.

Mosle, S. (2016). The new high-school outsiders. *New York Times Magazine*. Retrieved from http://www.nytimes.com/interactive/2016/09/11/magazine/refugee-studentsboise.html?_r=0.

Mustafa, N. (2017). *The girl from Aleppo: Nujeen's escape from war to freedom*. New York: HarperCollins.

O'Connor, J. (2015, December 20). Nujeen Mustafa: "Sometimes it's good to be unaware. Maybe I was too young to realise the danger." *The Guardian*. Retrieved from https://www.theguardian.com/world/2015/dec/20/nujeen-mustafa-interview-syrian-refugee.

Office of the High Commissioner Human Rights. (2018). Questions and answers about IDPs. Retrieved from https://www.ohchr.org/en/issues/idpersons/pages/issues.aspx.

Office of Refugee Resettlement. (n.d.). Find resources and contacts in your state. Retrieved from https://www.acf.hhs.gov/orr/state-programs-annual-overview.

Operation Pedro Pan Group. (2009). History: The Cuban children's exodus. Retrieved from http://www.pedropan.org/category/history.

Quinn, C. (Producer), & Quinn, C. & Walker, T. (Directors). (2006). *God grew tired of us: The story of lost boys of Sudan* [Motion picture]. United States: National Geographic Films.

Schwartz, E. (Producer), & Falardeau, P. (Director). (2014). *The good lie* [Motion picture]. United States: Alcon Entertainment.

TEDx. (2017, May 12). I am not a number: A refugee's tale. Retrieved from https://www.youtube.com/watch?v=R3r4gnSouqQ.

UNHCR. (2018). Figures at a glance. Retrieved from http://www.internal-displacement.org/global-report/grid2017/.

UNHCR. (2018). Teaching about refugees. Retrieved from http://www.unhcr.org/teaching-about-refugees.html.

UNHCR. (2018). US resettlement agencies. Retrieved from http://www.unhcr.org/en-us/us-resettlement-agencies.html.

United States Department of State. (2016). Fact sheet: Fiscal year 2016 refugee admissions. Retrieved from http://www.state.gov/r/pa/prs/ps/2016/10/262776.htm.

USHMM. (n.d.). Kindertransport 1938–1940. Retrieved from https://www.ushmm.org/wlc/en/article.php?ModuleId=10005260.

vlogbrothers. (2015, September 8). Understanding the refugee crisis in Europe, Syria, and around the world. Retrieved from https://www.youtube.com/watch?v=KVV6_1Sef9M.

7

WOMEN'S RIGHTS

Many people in the United States believe that women's rights[1] are a social problem of the past. The Nineteenth Amendment of the US Constitution ratified in 1920 guarantees women the right to vote and was extended by the Voting Rights Act of 1965 to include women from racially minoritized groups. The Equal Pay Act of 1963 called for equivalent earnings for women and men for the same labor, and the historic *Roe v. Wade* case of 1973 established the ability of women to make choices regarding their own bodies. Policies such as Title IX protect women from discrimination based on sex in any federally funded education program or activity. Furthermore, there are women serving in Congress, running multimillion-dollar corporations, and earning advanced degrees in a variety of disciplines. So, it would seem women are doing well and their rights are guaranteed. Why then, does society need to continue to talk about women's rights?

Despite the gains catalogued above, the oppression of women through systemic structures continues in overt and veiled ways. Like many other systems of oppression, years of subjugation cannot be easily erased with the passage of a few laws or bills. Gender inequity can be seen in a number of areas. For example, in 2016, "women working full time in the United States typically were paid just 80 percent of what men were paid" (Miller, 2018), and women are not projected to reach pay equal to men until the year 2119. Furthermore, in a nationally representative survey of two thousand people, 81 percent of women attested to having experienced sexual harassment and/or assault in their lifetime ("2018 Study," 2018).

The US Equal Employment Opportunity Commission reported hearing testimony that "one in four women face harassment in the workplace" ("Women in the American Workforce," 2015, para. 9).

Thus, gender inequity persists in both financial earnings as well as in the overall treatment of women. Even further, the National Sexual Violence Resource Center reports "91% of victims of rape and sexual assault are female" ("Get Statistics," 2018, para. 1). Women are being attacked at disturbing rates. And, perhaps surprisingly, the Equal Rights Amendment approved by Congress in 1972 remains yet to have been ratified by the number of states required to enact federal sanction. Thus, while equal rights may seem axiomatic for women, they are in fact not legally guaranteed.

These alarming numbers illustrate that women's rights are very much a thriving social problem that affect not only women, but all members of society. As leaders of the Women's March, a movement undertaken in 2017 that garnered massive support nationwide, avowed, "women's rights are human rights" ("Guiding Vision," 2017, para. 5), and thus warrant the attention of all citizens. The safety of all individuals in our society should be guaranteed, as should access to health care. No one should feel threatened in public spaces such as school or work. Youth, who are especially impacted by gender expectations and stereotypes, must consider, explore, and wrestle with the history and current aspects of women's rights so that they can disrupt harmful manifestations of gender oppression and enact more positive policies, actions, and attitudes. In this chapter, we use the novel *Gabi, a Girl in Pieces* by Isabel Quintero (2014) as a means for focusing students' attention on the crucial social concerns surrounding women's rights.

GABI, A GIRL IN PIECES

Told in diary entries through the powerful, comedic voice of a Latina female, *Gabi, a Girl in Pieces* traces the protagonist's various experiences coming of age. Gabi has two best friends featured prominently throughout the novel: Cindy, who becomes pregnant (as the result, readers learn late in the novel, of date rape) and deals with her family's and peers' reactions; and Sebastian, who identifies as a gay male and struggles in an unsupportive family situation. As Gabi helps her friends navigate their own issues, she deals with her Catholic mother's expectations for women, especially as they are related to interactions with men. Her mother's saying, "'Ojos abiertos, piernas cerradas.' Eyes open, legs closed" (p. 7), along with societal standards for women, follow Gabi throughout the novel as she positions these ideals alongside her own desires. Over the course of the novel, she has multiple encounters with adolescent males, including two boyfriends. With one of them, Martin, she falls in love and has sex, embracing her own womanhood.

Throughout the novel, readers also witness the impact of Gabi's father's drug addiction, which ultimately claims his life, on Gabi and her family. Despite his attempts at sobriety and Gabi's wishes that he would return to his "real" self (p. 31), "the beast" (p. 128) of substance abuse wins, and Gabi discovers her father in their garage after he has overdosed. Readers are also privy to Gabi's role in her enemy-turned-peer Georgina's abortion, in which Gabi agrees to help because of Georgina's sharing that her father, who is a Jehovah's Witness and physically abusive, would "really kill me" (p. 176).

In addition, Gabi recounts her endless battle with her own weight, for which her mother serves as a catalyst, and wonders if she is "too fat to look at naked" (p. 143). Finally, Gabi grapples with her desire to attend college despite pressure from her family to stay at home and serve in the role of a supportive daughter, especially since her father left her mother pregnant when he died and there is therefore a newborn baby in the family. Gabi, however, desperate to advance her education and break the confining molds she faces, is admitted to Berkeley and must choose her own path.

We chose this book to facilitate students' discussion and actions on women's rights because it reflects a wide range of concerns related to the topic and presents them through the lens of a strong narrator whose voice is witty, insightful, and inquisitive.

TEACHING STRATEGIES

Before Reading

Gabi's narrative offers a host of women's issues to explore, and we recommend beginning by exploring the history of women's rights in the

United States to provide a context for students. Some may feel, as the opening of this chapter suggests, that such a focus in not necessary and thus it will be important to make the case that there remain, in fact, many facets of this area to be acted upon. Students could conduct research and create a visual timeline of pertinent issues related to women's voting, reproductive, and labor rights, and then they could match those with the fronts along which women are still fighting today, using the Women's March website ("Guiding Vision," 2017) as a foundation for that information. Teachers could also divide students into groups according to specific areas such as those outlined above (sexual harassment or assault, voting rights, reproductive rights) and have them compose research presentations to share with the class, employing a jigsaw strategy through which they educate their peers on relevant topics.

Students could also view the film *Battle of the Sexes* (Dayton, Faris, Colson, Boylen, & Graf, 2017), a movie that recreates the story of the 1973 tennis match between Billie Jean King and Bobby Riggs. The film demonstrates many of the gender issues of its context, especially as they apply to sports. Students could research the actual match, the time period, and the key players. They could also compare the topics related to male chauvinism raised in the film to today's era and toxic masculinity.

As a further introduction to the concerns raised by women's rights, students can also explore expectations and gender roles. (See also chapter 4 on the gender spectrum.) They might first generate their own lists of stereotypes and/or expectations of women versus men and then be prompted to consider the origins of these, with teachers asking questions such as: *From where do our ideals of men and women come? How are these communicated to us?*

Teachers can then engage students in a critical analysis of media, first scaffolding their understandings by deconstructing advertisements and commercials that uphold gender stereotypes. They could begin with older posters that blatantly illustrate gender roles, such as the Kenwood Chef advertisement from 1961 that reads, "The Chef does everything but cook—that's what wives are for!" (The Advertising Archives, 1990) and transition to more modern-day examples such as a Gap advertisement that featured a young boy and girl in different clothing, with the girl labeled as "The Social Butterfly" and the boy labeled "The Little Scholar" (Kennedy, 2016). Teachers can ask: *What message does this advertisement communicate about women? About men? Why does it matter?*

Students might also view the clip in which NFL player Cam Newton laughs at a woman reporter who asks him about routes, stating that it was "funny" to hear a woman talk about routes (The Fumble, 2017). Teachers might ask students: *Why would Newton have found her question comical? How was Newton's response harmful? How is it reflective behavior we see in our daily lives?* Students might then read Jourdan Rodrigue's response on Twitter, which was later complicated by racist remarks uncovered in the reporter's past (Blavity Team, 2017). This could be an opportunity for teachers to further discuss notions of intersectionality and systems of oppression, emphasizing that while systems overlap, awareness in one area does not automatically lend itself to cognizance in another.

Students can additionally view clips from Jean Kilbourne's "Killing Us Softly" on YouTube (Openedmieyez, 2018), in which she catalogues years of advertisements and the damages they can cause. Finally, educators can highlight attempts to disrupt such negative portrayals, such as the Always commercial aired during the Super Bowl in 2015 (Always, 2015), and students can read about it in the Huffington Post article "The Reaction to #LikeAGirl Is Exactly Why It's So Important" (Vagianos, 2015). Teachers can ask students to analyze the effectiveness of such campaigns. They might also bring in examples of current figures, such as musicians and actors/actresses who defy gender stereotypes like Janelle Monáe or Miley Cyrus or who seek to champion the rights of all individuals like Lady Gaga or Ashley Judd. Students can examine specifically how those individuals are working against this system of oppression.

Finally, students might also consider how culture impacts expectations for women. Teachers can remind students that culture encompasses geography, religion, ethnicity, and generation. Caution is advised so as to avoid stereotyping cultures, but it will be important for students to discern how many cultures do contain divisions along gender lines. Students can consider how individuals are impacted through reading personal narratives such as "Beautiful and Cruel" from Sandra Cisneros's *House on Mango Street* (1984) and discussing how gender stereotypes are internalized and battled. They might also read the United Nations interview with Malala Yousafzai during which she discusses women's rights to an education and her own battles for the cause (UN News, 2017). Students could then compose their own journal entries about family expectations of them that might reveal gender roles and share if they wish.

During Reading

As students begin the text, they will be exposed immediately to Gabi's mother's expectations for her as a girl and should be able to directly relate those to the pre-reading activities. Mentioned previously, Gabi's mother's motto is, "'Ojos abiertos, piernas cerradas.' Eyes open, legs closed" (Quintero, 2014, p. 7). Her emphasis on abstinence and how girls "should" behave are made explicit multiple times in Gabi's interactions with her: for example, she says that girls should avoid being "easy, sluts, hoes, or ofrecidas. And that being this way was what got Cindy in trouble" (p. 106); "she says that girls are never free. They always have to comportarse bien. Behave well" (p. 107). She blames Cindy for becoming pregnant, placing the entire responsibility on her without regard for German, the boy who got Cindy pregnant. In another instance, she reminds Gabi that a different girl who became pregnant "was always wearing . . . short shorts. . . . Offering her goodies to everyone" (p. 34). She tells Gabi that all men want is sex, which causes Gabi to wonder if "my mom really thinks that all of our worth is between our legs. Once a man has access to that, then we are worth nothing, and there is no future for us" (p. 146).

Teachers can draw upon these examples to discuss with students differing perspectives on how women "should" act, drawing upon their previous conversations and comparing those with Gabi's mother's as they read them. Teachers might ask students: *Why would Gabi's mother think Cindy is to blame for becoming pregnant? Why might Gabi's mother not find German responsible also? How does she reflect broader narratives of victim blaming, and what can be done to alter those views? What does her mother mean when she says that girls are never free, and to what extent is this true or false?*

Gabi's mother's views extend also into what she expects of her daughter specifically as a Latina female, harkening back to how such notions can be culturally influenced. She believes that "good Mexican girls never turn away their parents, no matter how awful they've been" (p. 88). Gabi recognizes that her mother's own background likely influences her opinions, as she says:

> It's probably hard for her to have been raised in some pueblo in the
> 1970s where being good at housework and being pure were seen as
> necessary traits for being married—because that's what you were sup-
> posed to aspire to do. So it's even harder (I'm guessing) to raise a

Mexican-American daughter in Southern California in the 2000s, a girl who thinks that being good at housework and having an intact hymen are totally overrated. (p. 275)

Again, teachers can emphasis in conversation how gender expectations are complicated by culture and socialization. It will be important not to dismiss Gabi's mother as too traditional but rather to attempt to understand her and to brainstorm ways that Gabi might navigate the situation with her mother.

As students discuss these perspectives, they will undoubtedly also bring in broader societal expectations of men and women, which Gabi also catalogues. For instance, in her zine (pp. 195–202), Gabi includes an image of "proper good girl sitting procedure" (p. 201). Teachers might ask students to analyze the images presented in the zine, noting what messages Gabi is speaking against and how she does so through her artwork. Students will likely need an overview and definition of a zine, and they could research other pieces of art or media in which people have communicated messages of protest. Students could, for example, discuss Shepard Fairey's "We the People" inauguration posters and read the *Time* magazine article explaining their intent (Silva, 2017). Readers could consider questions such as: *How does Gabi deliver her message through the visual? How is the combination of words and images effective? Why wouldn't Gabi's teacher allow her to share her zine with the class?*

Not only does Gabi call into question the expectations placed upon her as a girl, but she continuously defies those standards. She kisses Eric, her first boyfriend, in the hallway, after which she notes, "Things were out of order—I was supposed to wait for him" (p. 54). Later, she again is the first to kiss her next boyfriend, Martin. In this situation, she shares, "I KISSED HIM. I broke one of the cardinal rules of being a girl. Again. I didn't wait for the boy to make the first move" (p. 138). In both instances, her male counterparts were surprised—as was Gabi—despite the fact that she acted upon her desires.

While reading these scenes, students can speculate what the sort of unwritten rules for dating are and how these are not only gendered but also heteronormative, as society typically reserves such rules for heterosexual couples. They might also consider if these are still as strict today as maybe they once were, or to what extent the rules of dating have changed, and, if so, how. In their conversation, teachers can prompt students to consider their own school and how dates for prom, for example, are secured. They could also ask how two students might end up going on a date, prompting youth with: *Who asks whom? How? Who pays? Why is it this way? What could be some alternatives?*

Despite Gabi's initial misgivings or worries about her impulsive actions, she becomes more confident in her decisions as the novel progresses. After having sex with Martin and arriving home very late on prom night, she notes, "I was feeling content. Am I a bad girl because I don't feel that guilty? Probably. But the thing is, I am starting to care less about that badness" (p. 248). Gabi's turn provides an opportunity for students to consider morals related to sex and how those also might be gendered.

A teacher might ask at this point in the novel: *Does society hold different views of men and women who engage in sex? Why?* Gabi calls attention to the double standards in our society, specifically through how her mother treats her brother Beto, feeling she "let him slide. She has expected less of him, and he has realized this" (p. 80), and how Joshua Moore, who had sex with Georgina, would not be "labeled slut and baby killer" (p. 204) if Georgina's abortion became known. Gabi even includes a list of "instructions for understanding what *boys will be boys* really means" (p. 229) and records various examples of how men get away with mistreatment of women and their behavior is dismissed. Teen readers might consider how such double standards and affordances exist in their own lives and schools, perhaps making their own lists similar to Gabi's.

The issue of consent is also worthy of focus as students read. Although Cindy says she became pregnant after having sex with German, she later admits that German in fact raped Cindy in the back of his mom's car. As Gabi recounts, Cindy told her friends she "was all for it at first, but then she changed her mind, and he said that she had already said yes, and she couldn't say no and that was that" (p. 229). While Gabi is furious, teachers might prompt students to consider Cindy's viewpoint and ask: *Why did Cindy not speak up sooner? What aspects of the situation made her uncertain about it? What is consent? How is it illustrated?*

To help facilitate their understandings, students might view the short film "What Is Consent?" (Health & Physical Education, 2016), which explains the concept of consent through a metaphor of a cup of tea. The video raises points about people's physical and emotional states as well as their rights to change their mind. It also covers how a person might want one thing one day and another on a different day and that those choices must be respected. Students can analyze Cindy's experience from the lens of the lessons in the video.

Readers might express some ambivalence because, as Cindy shares, German "didn't hit her or treat her badly, but he held her down, and she cried the whole time" (Quintero, 2014, p. 229). The situation therefore contradicts the way that sexual assault is often portrayed in media and thus perhaps confused Cindy. Some students might feel as Cindy does, and thus is it crucial to unpack consent even more and to emphasize the ways that sexual assault can manifest. Students might research statistics related to date rape and even, if appropriate, read personal narratives that are similar to Cindy's so they can see that hers is not an anomaly. For example, they might read and discuss Emily Doe's letter (Kingkade, 2016), the survivor of Brock Turner's assault.

Later too, Gabi catches herself thinking, "'He's too hot to force someone to sleep with him'. . . people wouldn't believe that he would 'have to' rape someone" (Quintero, 2014, pp. 258–259). This again reflects a broader cultural narrative, mistaking sexual assault as only about intercourse when really it reflects power and the imposition of one's will over another. Students might read about any host of famous men who have been indicted for harassment and assault, such as Matt Lauer or Larry Nassar, men who seemingly had wealth and fame but nonetheless committed atrocious acts against women. Students could use this knowledge to create posters or digital graphics defining sexual harassment and warning others against this dominant cultural narrative.

While German is an example of what *not* to do, Martin serves as his character foil. He is kind, patient, and sensitive. He shares with Gabi that his father told him, "I have to respect you and not pressure you to do things you don't want to do, and if you say no, it's no" (p. 255). Students can analyze the two male characters and how their different actions led to different consequences. They might take note of how Martin ensures his and Gabi's safety and comfort while German's actions changed Cindy's life forever.

Diverse consequences of sex are thus seen in the novel. While Cindy becomes pregnant and has a baby, Georgina becomes pregnant and has an abortion, and still Gabi has sex, uses protection, does not become pregnant, and continues in a healthy relationship with Martin. Quintero juxtaposes the birth of Cindy's baby in a chapter almost next to that of Georgina's abortion. While teachers will have to utilize discretion according to their teaching context, it would be worthwhile to note these scenarios with students.

Gabi discloses of Cindy's labor that she "can't understand how something so utterly disgusting can be so utterly beautiful at the same time" (p. 173). In true Gabi fashion, she does not romanticize the details of birth, sharing "we had all just seen her vagina" and "witnessed her pooping" (p. 174). In the next section, she treats Georgina's predicament with care and concern, stating, "I know she feels bad about it. Really bad. But she doesn't have another choice or feels like she doesn't have another choice" (p. 182). She even notes, "It had never occurred to me that strength was needed to make this choice" (p. 182). Both the birth and abortion, then, are approached as the significant events that they are, allowing students to grapple with the magnitude of each. Teachers might ask: *Why does Georgina feel her only choice is abortion? What are the long-term effects for both her and Cindy? How is Gabi understanding and sympathetic to each?*

Finally, Gabi has an encounter with German at the end of the novel in which she confronts him about his assault of Cindy. She physically attacks German and is suspended from school for doing so, all the while not disclosing the true motivation for her actions and maintaining her silence around the rape. Students may have a difficult time understanding how Cindy could be mad at her friend after this incident, despite the fact that Gabi herself comes to discern what would have been a better approach— "what I should have done . . . was to just be there for her and suggest she talk to someone (a teacher, the police, a counselor)" (p. 269). In order to help students ruminate on these deeply complex moral issues, teachers might ask: *Should Gabi have punched German? How could she have helped Cindy once she learned the truth about what happened?* Students could then rewrite either the scene with Gabi and German in the cafeteria or the conversation between Gabi and Cindy to imagine how it could have gone differently.

After Reading

Once students finish the novel and have discussed these complicated themes, they should be encouraged to research the laws and policies regarding women's rights and sexual assault as they are represented in the novel. They could investigate what Cindy's rights are and how she could go about getting justice if she chose to do so. They might also look further into the issue of consent and what the surrounding policies are in their state, even perhaps reading statements composed on college campuses where this has become of extreme import. One such statement from the University of North Carolina at Chapel Hill instructs individuals to "Think A.C.E. for consent—100% agreement (freely made and conscious decision), communicated clearly (words and/or actions), every time" (University of North Carolina, 2018). Students could also read court cases such as those related to the Steubenville High School rape case or Brock Turner's and determine if they feel justice was served.

Students might also look further into the #metoo movement and those individuals who have spoken out. They could invite a guest speaker to their class to further present on these issues and answer questions they have. They could also look further into any legislation that governs sexual harassment and assault in schools and what protections exist to ensure their safety and the safety of others.

In order to help students think more deeply about how Gabi's experience reflects a feminist narrative, teachers could task students with researching the various waves of feminism and applying the principles of each to Gabi's experience and perspectives. They might do this in small groups, with different waves assigned to groups and then teach one another. Or, they could read a source that represents each wave, keeping track in a graphic organizer of the major principles of each and then noting similar examples from the novel. They could read Sojourner Truth's 1851 "Ain't I a Woman" (Podell, n.d.) and Susan B. Anthony's speech from 1872 (History Place, n.d.) as representative of the focus on the first wave on women's suffrage. A selection from Betty Friedan's *The Feminine Mystique* (1963) would illustrate the emphasis on women's personal lives in the second wave, as would Helen Reddy's song, "I Am Woman," to which students could listen and analyze the lyrics. They might also examine Title IX, passed in 1972 as a statute of the Education Amendments, which states, "No person in the United States shall, on the basis of sex, be excluded from participation in, be denied the benefits of, or be subjected to discrimination under any education program or activity receiving Federal financial assistance" (Office for Civil Rights, 2015).

Third wave feminism, beginning in the 1990s, responded to the second wave's exclusion of women of color and lesbian women. Students, provided with the context for Rebecca Walker's article as a reaction to

Clarence Thomas's appointment as a Supreme Court judge despite being accused of sexual harassment, could read "Becoming the Third Wave" (Walker, 1992). This document, combined with listening to Destiny's Child's song "Independent Women," would give students a sense of the focus on social issues and diversity relevant to the third wave.

The most recent wave of feminism, not wholly agreed upon as separate from the third but growing in recognition, brings women's rights and feminist critiques into the public spotlight through social media. Students could read Sophie Gilbert's article "The Movement of #MeToo: How a Hashtag Got Its Power" (2017) to learn about the genesis of the effort and its trajectory. They could read about the current status and mission of the movement on its website ("me too," 2018) and explore the resources particularly for youth.

To extend their understandings of feminism, students can locate historic and contemporary feminists (e.g., Gloria Steinem, Angela Davis, Coretta Scott King, Patricia Arquette, or Shonda Rimes) who adhere to the messages promoted in *Gabi, a Girl in Pieces* and research their stories and activism. They can consider how culture influences each and note differences in generation and ethnicity when considering the goals of present-day feminists. It will also be important to discuss misconceptions and misapplications of feminism today, as many, upon hearing this *f* word, are quick to reject it as an outdated or radical term. Montclair Diplomats' "The Misconception about Feminism" (Sacirbey, 2016) is a resource that explains what feminism is, and Villanova University's website "Myths and Truths about Feminism" (Hughes, Cardiel, & Cardiel, n.d.) includes an overview of how feminism helps women *and* men. From these resources, students could create visuals of the definitions of feminism to ensure better understandings.

Expanding on their examination of how the book represents a feminist outlook, students might propose alternative titles that capture one related element they feel is most outstanding. They could then design a new book cover and justify it based on their analysis of the waves represented throughout the novel and the focus. For example, the notion of reproductive rights is predominant in the novel, and students might wish to capitalize on that perspective; they might instead emphasize body image and Gabi's struggle to see herself positively; or, they could highlight the issue of consent and the silence around sexual assault. As there are a multitude of aspects related to women in the text, students could create around any one with which they are most comfortable.

IDEAS FOR SOCIAL ACTION

Once students have conducted the above research and wrestled with the topics broached in the text, there are multiple avenues they could take for action. They could design their own zines related to gender roles or other societal expectations to which they might like to speak back. Scholastic houses a helpful resource for teachers, ZineMaking 101 (DePasquale, 2016), and another for students that provides step-by-step directions and pictures is on the Rookie Mag website (Dajska, 2012). Teachers could combine all student work into one publishable document to share with the school and community.

Students might also design campaigns advocating language awareness to reduce microaggressions experienced by women in our culture as well as more overt forms of sexual harassment. This could include creating posters and/or memes to post on social media to circulate their messages. Our culture is so ingrained with normalized language patterns as simple as saying "hey guys," that drawing attention to such uses is necessary and is an action that students could easily accomplish. As a catalyst for thinking about the normalization of language, teachers could watch the clip in which tennis player Andy Murray corrects a reporter with "first male player" when the journalist says he was battling against "the first US player" to make it to the semifinal of a Grand Slam match since 2009 (WXYZ-TV, 2017).

While a seemingly small verbal omission, students might speculate on the importance of the language used, noting how women's sports are often referred to with that terminology while men's are not preceded by gender (e.g., women's soccer versus soccer). Along these lines, students might also create public service announcements to educate their peers on these verbal slights and share these videos widely.

An extension of school-level intervention could be that students investigate their institution's policies on sexual harassment and/or dress codes and determine if these should be revised or updated given more recent movements and fourth wave feminism. If they determine such actions are needed, they could present their case and any recommendations to their administration or school board. They might also propose, if their school does not have a procedure in place, a reporting system and outline steps to take if someone is sexually harassed or assaulted. Publicizing such guidelines in spaces easily accessible to students, such as the cafeteria or main office, would be key to spreading information effectively.

Other students might be interested in efforts to pass the Equal Rights Amendment and might write or even meet with their local government officials, presenting researched arguments as to why this legislation is still important. They might undertake efforts to enhance the positive body image of women in their school, posting uplifting and affirming messages in hallways and other spaces such as bulletin boards. To create these, they could research and draw upon strong women in history and in their current era, such as female fighter pilots, athletes, or lawmakers. They could even use strong women in their school or local community.

Another action project might be for students to envision what a "fifth wave" of feminism might bring and to attempt to begin that movement themselves. Teachers might challenge students to consider: *If the fourth wave brought feminist critique and attention to assailants to the public eye, how might an additional wave work to address grievances, work toward social justice, and bring down toxic masculinity? What steps would need to be taken to get to a society in which women are no longer assaulted or harassed?*

Finally, embracing the latter waves of feminism, students might endeavor to spread acceptance of various types of women and the inclusion of those on the spectrum of sexual orientations and gender expression, including those who identify as transgender or lesbian (see chapter 11 on sexual orientations and stigmas). They might form a club in which all students are welcome to address equity in their schools or envision informative events where these issues are explained. There are therefore a multitude of ways teachers can work with students to advance the rights of women, educate themselves and their peers on issues in which women are mistreated, and bring attention to the opportunities that exist for bettering this aspect of society.

SUPPLEMENTAL RESOURCES

Canonical Companions

The Scarlet Letter by Nathaniel Hawthorne
The Color Purple by Alice Walker
The Bell Jar by Sylvia Plath
Their Eyes Were Watching God by Zora Neale Hurston

Connected Young Adult Literature

The Nowhere Girls by Amy Reed
Speak by Laurie Halse Anderson
Uprising by Margaret Peterson Haddix

Connected Music

"I Am Woman" by Helen Reddy
"Independent Women" by Destiny's Child

NOTE

1. We uphold the notion that the gender binary is a false dichotomy and support the spectrum along which gender exists. Given that there are lived social consequences of this binary, however, we focus this chapter on exploring those with students.

REFERENCES

2018 study on sexual harassment and assault. (2018). Stop Street Harassment. Retrieved from http://www.stopstreetharassment.org/resources/2018-national-sexual-abuse-report/.
The Advertising Archives. (1990). Retrieved from http://www.advertisingarchives.co.uk/detail/14356/1/Magazine-Advert/Kenwood-Chef/1960s.
Always. (2015, January 29). Always #LikeaGirl-Super Bowl XLIX [Video file]. Retrieved from https://www.youtube.com/watch?v=yIxA3o84syY.
Blavity Team. (2017). Sports writer at the center of Cam Newton controversy caught being racist online: Watch white feminism work. *Blavity*. Retrieved from https://blavity.com/breaking-sports-writer-at-the-center-of-cam-newton-controversy-caught-being-racist-online.

Cisneros, S. (1984). *The house on Mango Street.* Houston, TX: Arte Público Press.

Dajska, E. (2012, May 1). How to make a zine. Retrieved from http://www.rookiemag.com/2012/05/how-to-make-a-zine/.

Dayton, J. & Faris, V. (Producers) & Colson, C., Boyle, D., & Graf, R. (Directors). (2017). *Battle of the sexes* [Motion picture]. United States: Fox Searchlight Pictures.

DePasquale, J. (2016, April 29). Zine making 101. Retrieved from https://www.scholastic.com/teachers/blog-posts/john-depasquale/zine-making-101/.

Friedan, B. (1963). *The feminine mystique.* New York: W. W. Norton.

The Fumble. (2017, October 5). Cam Newton laughs at female reporter for talking about wide receiver routes [Video file]. Retrieved from https://www.youtube.com/watch?v=mZtK7d2p5Dg.

Get statistics: Sexual assault in the United States. (2018). National Sexual Violence Resource Center. Pennsylvania Coalition Against Rape. Retrieved from https://www.nsvrc.org/statistics.

Gilbert, S. (2017, October 16). The movement of #MeToo: How a hashtag got its power. *The Atlantic.* Retrieved from https://www.theatlantic.com/entertainment/archive/2017/10/the-movement-of-metoo/542979/.

Guiding vision and definition of principles. (2017). Women's March on Washington. Retrieved from https://static1.squarespace.com/static/584086c7be6594762f5ec56e/t/587ffb20579fb3554668c111/1484782369253/WMW+Guiding+Vision+%26+Definition+of+Principles.pdf.

Health & Physical Education. (2016). What is consent? [Video File]. Retrieved from https://www.teachertube.com/video/what-is-consent-422016.

History Place: Great Speeches Collection. (n.d.) Susan B. Anthony on women's right to vote. Retrieved from http://www.historyplace.com/speeches/anthony.htm.

Hughes, K., Cardiel, J., & Cardiel, C. (n.d.). Myths and truths about feminism. Villanova University Liberal Arts and Sciences. Retrieved from https://www1.villanova.edu/villanova/artsci/gws/resources/myths.html.

Kennedy, M. (2016, August 1). Gap accused of sexism over "social butterfly" children's T-shirt ad. *The Guardian.* Retrieved from https://www.theguardian.com/fashion/2016/aug/01/gap-accused-sexism-social-butterfly-pink-childrens-t-shirt.

Kingkade, T. (2016). Stanford victim letter impact statement from Brock Turner's victim. *The Huffington Post.* Retrieved from https://www.documentcloud.org/documents/2852615-Stanford-Victim-Letter-Impact-Statement-From.html.

"me too." (2018). Retrieved from https://metoomvmt.org/.

Miller, K. (2018). The simple truth about the gender pay gap. The American Association of University Women. Retrieved from https://www.aauw.org/research/the-simple-truth-about-the-gender-pay-gap/.

Office for Civil Rights. (2015). Title IX and sex discrimination. U.S. Department of Education. Retrieved from https://www2.ed.gov/about/offices/list/ocr/docs/tix_dis.html.

Openedmieyez. (2018, February 7). Killing us softly 4 advertising's image of women [Video file]. Retrieved from https://www.youtube.com/watch?v=xnAY6S4_m5I.

Podell, L. (n.d.) Compare the two speeches. The Sojourner Truth Project. Retrieved from https://www.thesojournertruthproject.com/compare-the-speeches/.

Quintero, I. (2014). *Gabi, a girl in pieces.* El Paso: Cinco Puntos Press.

Sacirbey, S. (2016, May 17). The misconception about feminism. *The Huffington Post.* Retrieved from https://www.huffingtonpost.com/montclair-diplomats/the-misconception-about-f_b_9959932.html.

Silva, B. (2017, January 19). The story behind Shepard Fairey's inauguration protest posters. *Time.* Retrieved from http://time.com/4639618/trump-inauguration-shepard-fairey/.

UN News. (2017, April 11). In new UN role, Malala Yousafzai seeks to inspire girls to stand up, speak out for rights. Retrieved from https://news.un.org/en/story/2017/04/555182-interview-new-un-role-malala-yousafzai-seeks-inspire-girls-stand-speak-out.

University of North Carolina at Chapel Hill: Workforce Strategy, Equity and Engagement Equal Opportunity and Compliance. (2018). Policy on prohibited discrimination, harassment and related misconduct. Retrieved from https://eoc.unc.edu/our-policies/ppdhrm/.

Vagianos, A. (2015, Feburary 3). The reaction to #LikeaGirl is exactly why it's so important. *The Huffington Post.* Retrieved from https://www.huffingtonpost.com/2015/02/03/why-like-a-girl-is-so-important_n_6598970.html.

Walker, R. (1992, January). Becoming the third wave. *Ms. Magazine.* Retrieved from http://www.msmagazine.com/spring2002/BecomingThirdWaveRebeccaWalker.pdf.

Women in the American Workforce. (2015). U.S. Equal Employment Opportunity Commission. Retrieved from https://www.eeoc.gov/eeoc/statistics/reports/american_experiences/women.cfm.

WXYZ-TV Detroit, Channel 7. (2017, July 12). "Male player!" Andy Murray corrects reporter at Wimbledon [Video file]. Retrieved from https://www.youtube.com/watch?v=wOH-dCrV_XA.

8

SOCIAL CLASS DISPARITIES
IN THE UNITED STATES

According to data from the 2016 US Census Bureau, 12.7 percent of people (43.1 million) are living in poverty. Over a quarter of those, approximately fifteen million, are children. In fact, 21 percent of all children "live in families with incomes below the federal poverty threshold, a measurement that has been shown to underestimate the needs of families" (National Center for Children in Poverty, 2018, para. 1).

While the official poverty level in 2015 was $24,036 for a family of two adults and two children (Anne E. Casey, 2017), research shows that, on average, families need an income of about twice that level to cover basic expenses. Using this standard, 43 percent of children live in low-income families (NCCP, 2018). Moreover, there is a disparity among the poor with regard to race and ethnicity, with 12 percent of White children, 31 percent of Latinx children, and 36 percent of African American children living in families with limited incomes (Anne E. Casey, 2017).

Poverty abounds in communities across the United States, and opinions about those who struggle financially are not always favorable. Among the prevailing stereotypes of those who are poor are that they are lazy, uneducated, drug and alcohol abusers, and government moochers (e.g., Eichelberger, 2014; Gorski, 2008; Porter, 2015). To exacerbate stereotypes, many people believe the "pull yourself up by your bootstraps" mythology—that if people simply work hard enough, they can attain the "American Dream."

However, factors that contribute to poverty create situations much more complicated than these myths suggest. For example, according to the US Census Bureau, in 2012, "about 1.1 million people who made less than $25,000 a year, worked full time, and were heads of household and had a bachelor's degree" (Eichelberger, 2014). Thus, the notion that those who live in poverty are uneducated or unwilling to work is often untrue.

It's important for students to understand not only the complexity of and systemic factors that impact socioeconomic status, but also how social class affects people, as there are people who are struggling financially in every community across the United States and students will work and interact with those who have different economic needs than they do. Due to its prevalence, a unit of study on poverty should be easily accessible to all students; however, as students themselves may have economic challenges, teachers will want to be sensitive in their approach to discussions, being careful not to use othering or blaming language, and never requiring students to share their personal or family experiences and/or financial needs.

This chapter focuses on economic inequalities and their impacts on individuals and communities in the United States. Issues of systemic poverty in general and the unique considerations for those living in rural poverty in particular will be emphasized through a reading of Jeff Zentner's (2016) book *The Serpent King*.

THE SERPENT KING

Set in rural Tennessee, *The Serpent King* by Jeff Zentner (2016) explores issues of poverty, identity, love, and loss. The book alternates among three characters, Dill, Lydia, and Travis, who are all in their senior year of high school and considering their options for the future. Dill is the son of Pastor Early of the Church of Christ's disciples with Signs of Belief, a controversial and extremist sect of religion that encourages parishioners to "drink diluted battery acid and strychnine" (pp. 6–7) and handle copperheads and rattlesnakes as part of their worship services. Pastor Early is incarcerated for "possession of more than one hundred images depicting a minor engaged in sexual activity" (p. 7). With his father in prison, Dill feels an obligation to help support his mother financially.

Travis has plans to continue his current job with the family business, Bohannon Lumber, but finds escape in his beloved fantasy novels. Meanwhile, Lydia, while unpopular at her high school, has a wildly successful fashion blog and plans to move to New York City for college. Together the three support one another as they navigate high school in their rural town.

We chose this coming-of-age novel to be the focus of the chapter not only because it is beautifully written and emotionally moving, but also because its rural setting, not commonly found in YA novels that portray poverty (Darragh & Hill, 2014), offers students opportunities to consider what makes rural poverty unique from urban poverty and how they might develop social action projects to support families in need in their own communities as well as across the nation.

TEACHING STRATEGIES

Before Reading

Before leading a unit of study on poverty, teachers themselves will want to consider their own attitudes and beliefs about those with limited incomes. Specifically, teachers will want to consider what it means to *teach* students with limited incomes, and as such, Gorski's (2007) article, "The Question of Class," might be a good place to start. In identifying their own experiences, potential biases, and mis/perceptions, teachers will be better able to help their students to do the same.

There are many stereotypes regarding people who are poor. Teachers can help students identify their own beliefs and those in broader society regarding those who struggle financially. Once identified, teachers can work with students to unpack and locate from where those ideas originated, what has confirmed or supported those beliefs, and what they might do to combat any misinformation.

The Teaching Tolerance website offers a series of four lesson plans that are useful in introducing students to the complexity of poverty. The plans have:

> two overarching goals. First, the lessons aim to help students understand that poverty is systemic, rooted in economics, politics and dis-

crimination. Second, the lessons provide evidence to show that poverty, far from being random, disproportionately affects Americans who
have traditionally experienced oppression—African Americans, Lati-
nos, immigrants and children. (Teaching Tolerance, 1991–2018, para.
1)

For example, one of the lessons on the site suggests that, in groups,
students use a Cost of Living calculation sheet, identifying their perceived living needs, and then comparing those with the Federal Poverty
Guidelines. Students are prompted to consider what are essential needs,
like insurance, a car, and a cell phone. Then they look up the federal
minimum wage and determine if their living needs can be met earning
minimum wage and, if not, what would they choose to cut from their
original list.

Activities like these can help to dispel various pervasive myths surrounding poverty, like all people who are poor are lazy, don't have jobs,
and can easily get out of their situation if they just try. Other provided
lessons on the Teaching Tolerance website offer opportunities to look at
the cycle of poverty and the intersection of poverty and race as it plays
out in the United States today.

Similarly, the Family Consumer Sciences website offers lesson plans
and discussion prompts to help students begin to think critically about
poverty. Questions provided, such as *What do you think of when you hear
the word* poverty*? Where do we see poverty? How do people end up
living in poverty? Can you be employed and still be living at the poverty
level?* (n.d., para. 3), allow students to explore their beliefs before reading
a novel with poverty themes.

Along with these discussion questions, the Family and Consumer Sciences website also offers some activities to help students consider ongoing expenses (e.g., food, housing, health care, internet, pets). One such
activity suggests students work with a partner to determine which expenses from a provided list are necessary and which are "nonessential
extras." Students can extend this activity by brainstorming their own list
of expenses, then researching how much they would need to bring home
each month to meet their identified needs while keeping some money
aside for emergencies.

Teachers might also challenge students to play SPENT (2011), a free
online simulation game about poverty that walks students through some
difficult choices that they might have to make when it comes to spending

money. This is a way that students can independently consider what it means to struggle financially. While teachers should use caution in calling the simulation a "game," as that could lead to students not taking the activity seriously, it can be a valuable, eye-opening experience for students to see how costs add up and how one unexpected event (from a health problem to wanting to travel to attend a best friend's wedding) can lead to lacking income.

Hill and Darragh (2017) offer activities that can help students "increase awareness" about poverty, including a "Cross the Line" activity, a "Budget Your Day" activity, and links to a poverty quiz that students can take to test their knowledge regarding people who are struggling financially. In addition, a reading and discussion revolving around the editorial "What do we think poverty looks like?" (McMillan, 2017) can help students uncover prevailing misconceptions about the poor. Upon reading the article, teachers can ask students questions like, *How does the author address the intersection of race and poverty? How is poverty depicted in the media? What representations are missing from the media? What are the implications of seeing/not seeing one's poverty experience represented in the media?*

During Reading

While reading the novel, teachers can aid students in considering the challenges of living in poverty that are unique to various settings. For example, rural poverty, as exemplified in *The Serpent King*, has a specific set of challenges. With homes spread out and fewer people living in individual communities, access to public transportation, soup kitchens, and homeless shelters, among other supports, is less likely to exist.

While sometimes called "invisible poverty," as the general public may not traverse rural areas in financial struggle, the fact is that rural poverty is prevalent across the nation. According to the US Department of Agriculture:

> About one in four (23.5 percent) rural children in the United States were poor in 2016, compared to about one in five (20.5 percent) urban children. At the county level, on average between 2012 and 2016, there were 41 counties in the United States with child poverty rates of

50 percent or higher, 38 of which were rural (nonmetro) counties heavily clustered in the South (31 of these counties). (2018, para. 8)

Diane Sawyer's (ABC, 2009) series "A Hidden America: Children of the Mountains" provides some specific examples of the challenges of living in poverty in Appalachia. Each of the six segments, focusing on a different family, can be found on YouTube. Teachers can choose which segments they would like to show, following those up with discussion questions for students to consider.

To offer an alternate perspective, students can read Dotson-Lewis's (2009) article "Speak Your Piece: Diane Sawyer in Eastern Kentucky" and identify the specific issues the author has with the way people of Appalachia were depicted in this documentary. Teachers can prompt students to consider: *What is not shown about the people in the video clips? What do they perhaps* have *that those who are not economically challenged do not? What other stories could have been told to paint a fuller picture of the children of the mountains?* Activities like this can help to combat a deficit perspective regarding people who are poor. As a companion activity, if teachers use the YouTube videos, they can illustrate the negative stereotypes people who viewed the series have expressed with regard to the families in the segments.

While uncomfortable, having students read out loud some of the comments people made about the various clips (e.g., "get you GED, get off the smack and for the love of GOD do not get pregnant again!!! BTW I didn't watch the whole thing" and, "sat next to a guy on a greyhound bus a few years ago. He met a girl on the computer and went to presleysburg Kentucky to meet her. It was in the hills and the people were all criminals") can help demonstrate the stereotypes and negativity that abound regarding people who are poor. Students might want to contribute their own comments to dispel the negativity expressed, particularly considering *Does money make everything better? Can money buy happiness?*; and teachers can use the exercise to broach the topic of safe and respectful social media activity.

Students can explore how media promulgates negative stereotypes about poverty in general, and rural poverty in particular. For example, teachers can have students watch the local news and identify the following: *Is the story positive or negative? Who is interviewed? What are they wearing? Where does the interview take place? What is the unspoken message? What knowledges do the people have that aren't shown? How are those unseen knowledges valuable?* Students can each take a day for watching the evening news, analyzing the representations of people who are poor. Once they have charted out the information, they can compare their results to what they know about the characters in the novel and identify ways in which the media can help form opinions about people representing various economic groups.

While reading *The Serpent King*, there are opportunities for students to dispel the myths they might have about poverty through the characters of Dill and Travis. For example, a common misperception about people who are poor is that they mooch off the system and spend (hard-working taxpayer's money) government assistance on frivolous items like electronics and expensive clothing. Connected to the novel, teachers can ask questions to help students complicate these stereotypes, asking questions such as: *Dill has a computer and new school clothes. Is he rich? Is he bilking the system? What are the circumstances regarding these possessions?*

Another common stereotype is that people who are poor are lazy. Teachers can ask: *Is Dill's mom lazy? Where does she work? How has work impacted her family and her life—personally, physically, emotionally? What challenges does she face in keeping her job? Since she works, how is it that the family is still struggling financially?*

Regarding the myth that people who are poor do not value education, teachers can pose the following: *Does Dill value education? Why do you think his mom doesn't care if he drops out of school? What are the challenges Dill faces if he decides to pursue higher education?*

In addition to a discussion of poverty, teachers can encourage students to analyze the pros and cons of online personas versus face-to-face relationships. Lydia, Travis, and Dill all use social media in various ways. *In what ways does social media improve their lives, and in what ways does it add complications?* Students can rewrite scenes of the novel eliminating social media and analyzing the changes that would follow. They can also debate the pros and cons of social media use for teens today. Teachers can have students choose one side of the issue to research, then assign them the opposing side to research and debate, either verbally or in writing.

After Reading

Jeff Zentner is a singer-songwriter and guitarist, and students might be interested in listening to some of his music, analyzing the lyrics, and identifying songs they feel best connect to scenes in the novel. For example, "The Dying Days of Summer" and "If This Is to Be Goodbye" have obvious connections to the second half of the novel, and students can demonstrate their understanding of essential plot elements as well as the mood of characters/tone of the scenes through a musical analysis.

At various times in the novel, Lydia makes CDs for Dill, including songs from Arcade Fire, Fleet Foxes, Radiohead, New Order, Joy Division, Nick Cave & the Bad Seeds, Gun Club, and Leonard Cohen. Students can listen to the music and read various lyrics from these artists, identifying which songs they believe Lydia would put on a mix CD for Dill and explaining, with textual evidence, their choices. They might even add music from their own preferences and include justifications of their choices through song lyrics, drawing specific connections to scenes or lines from the novel.

For example, the song "Into My Arms" by Nick Cave (whom Lydia mentions in the novel) echoes the themes of religion and questioning faith that are developed in the book. Likewise, an analysis of "Meet Me by the River's Edge" by Gaslight Anthem can yield connections to the various scenes taking place at the Column, both when Lydia, Dill, and Travis write on the Column, and later when Lydia and Dill "listen(ed) to the river wear its way deeper into the Earth, the way people wear grooves into each other's hearts" (Zentner, p. 352). Finally, The Kinnardlys' song "Be Happy for Me" matches the simultaneous melancholy and excitement Dill and Lydia feel at the end of the novel as they embark upon new journeys and leave their old lives behind.

Also connected to music, the song "Love Will Tear Us Apart" by Joy Division is Lydia's "favorite song on Earth." Students can listen to the lyrics and discuss, using textual evidence to support their claims, why they think she likes this song so much. Following, they can identify their own "favorite song on Earth," sharing a clip of the music as well as why they like it and why they think it represents them well at this moment in time.

Throughout the book, Lydia cites quotes from Dolly Parton, and her blog, *Dollywould*, also pays tribute to Dolly, one of her role models.

Students can research the background of Dolly Parton, from her child-hood growing up poor in Tennessee to her Dollywood Foundation in general and the Imagination Library in particular. They can also choose someone they think would serve as a role model for Dill and and/or Travis and conduct further research, perhaps focusing on contributions those individuals made to support people in need. Or, they could choose a celebrity from their own state who is involved in various philanthropic work and investigate why this figure chooses to give to a particular community.

Also in conjunction with Lydia's blog, students can identify what makes a "good" blog by and/or for teens. They can survey classmates and other teens they know, and develop an evaluation tool for rating blogs, identifying some positive and negative examples, and sharing their findings with classmates, parents, and members of the community. Similarly, they can identify what the goal of their own personal blog would be if they were to start one. They can map out purpose, target audience, tone, and topics they could include—even actually creating the blog if they choose to do so.

Media in general and films in particular can help perpetuate ideas about poverty. After reading the novel, teachers can lead students in an analysis of films that portray poverty and homelessness. Students can create a class rubric for evaluation stereotypes and negative portrayals of poverty based on their reading and viewing thus far in the unit. They can read Pimpare's (2018) editorial, "Where Are All the Films about Poor Americans?," adding other films they can think of to the list and running each through the problematic portrayals identified in order to debate whether or not they agree with him.

For example, they can analyze the representations of poverty in *The Hunger Games* and the Harry Potter movies (the Weasley family is poor; Harry does not have disposable income), tracking if and how the characters represent common stereotypes about the poor, such as if they are lazy, make bad decisions, want handouts, and more.

IDEAS FOR SOCIAL ACTION

Students can identify local organizations that provide social services and interview them regarding their specific needs. Be it blankets, toys, snacks, and/or hygiene products, students can offer supports through fundraising. For example, in *The Serpent King*, Dill takes part in his school's talent show competition. Students can organize a school and/or community talent show asking for identified needed items and/or a donation of any amount as a recommendation (not requirement!) for admission.

Research shows that often parents with limited incomes are not involved with school due to work and familial responsibilities. Students can organize free child care to be available during parent/teacher conferences and meet-the-teacher nights. In addition, some communities have organized shopping events where they have solicited donations of gently used professional clothing and/or formal wear. People who need clothing for an interview and or an event like prom can choose items for free or for a nominal donation. Local businesses can get involved as well. For example, local barbershops, beauty salons, and/or cosmetology schools can offer haircuts and hair and nail styling as part of the event.

Students can also analyze the available resources in their own school and community, investigating what supports are available for those struggling financially and what gaps may exist. If there are gaps, students can then proffer how those gaps might be filled. For example, while all public schools offer free and reduced meals during the school year, students can research their own school districts to see if food supports are available on weekends, over the summer, and during holiday/inclement weather days.

Similarly, at various times in the novel, Lydia notices Dill's "unappetizing free lunch" (e.g., p. 185). Students can research what kind of funding is provided for free and reduced lunch as well as for the Supplemental Nutrition Assistance Program (SNAP), and identify potentially cost-effective healthy options for those receiving food supports. They can propose these options at a school board meeting or via a letter to the editor in the local newspaper.

For Dill's mother's birthday, he is able to secure a dented box of cake mix from the grocery store where he works. This scene in the book offers the opportunity for students to consider the challenges of celebrations for students whose families are unable to provide celebratory food or gifts. While various churches and community groups often offer support around Christmas, there often are not resources put aside for birthdays.

Students can brainstorm ways in which they might be able to help make birthdays special for all children in their local elementary school.

For example, at the first of each month, students can offer a "birthday party" for all of the students in the school who have a birthday that month. They can investigate potential community resources for donations (e.g., a local bakery for sweet treats, gently used party decorations, etc.) that they can use to make the day special, and even pair elementary students with high school students to make a birthday card—as a way to ensure that all students have their birthday celebrated.

It is important to note that the above examples focus on "giving." While this can be helpful, encouraged, and often makes the giver feel even better than the receiver, giving alone does not address the systemic components of poverty, nor ways in which to address the system and break the cycle, so those types of projects should also be encouraged.

For example, students can embark upon a mythbusting campaign in their schools and/or communities to debunk stereotypes surrounding poverty and highlight the systemic and cyclical nature of poverty in order to raise awareness. Posters, statistics, and scenarios can be used to dismantle stereotypes and illuminate how just one unexpected event (e.g., an illness, natural disaster, a layoff) can send someone into an economic state in which they cannot easily get out.

In regard to pursuing postsecondary education, Lydia has a strong support system from her parents, and she and they, in turn, support Dill. Students can identify the steps needed to be taken in order to apply for colleges and financial aid. They can also identify barriers to the process and brainstorm ways in which to overcome those barriers.

For example, perhaps the necessary paperwork is confusing. Students can work with guidance counselors and community members to set up a college application night, where guardians and teens can come and get assistance and have questions answered. High school students who are not participating in the workshop can offer free child care and a meal—alleviating some of the stress that attending an evening function can cause for working families. For students who are interested but do not have a parent or guardian able to come with them, perhaps they can be assigned a community volunteer for the evening.

Helping students to understand the complexity of poverty is the first step in combatting the systemic structures in place that make it so hard for people to become financially stable (see also chapter 2, Global Poverty). In identifying and developing their own social action projects connected to both their interests and their communities, students can begin to take steps in breaking down social class disparities in the United States.

SUPPLEMENTAL RESOURCES

Canonical Companions

The Good Earth by Pearl Buck
Great Expectations by Charles Dickens
A Tree Grows in Brooklyn by Betty Smith
The Grapes of Wrath by John Steinbeck

Connected Young Adult Literature

The Absolutely True Diary of a Part-Time Indian by Sherman Alexie
The Smell of Other People's Houses by Bonnie-Sue Hitchcock
The Hunger Games by Suzanne Collins
Shine by Lauren Myracle

Connected Music

"Into My Arms" by Nick Cave
"Meet Me by the River's Edge" by Gaslight Anthem
"Love Will Tear Us Apart" by Joy Division
"Be Happy for Me" by The Kinnardlys
"The Dying Days of Summer" by Jeff Zentner
"If This Is to Be Goodbye" by Jeff Zentner

REFERENCES

ABC News. (2009). Hidden America: Children of the mountains [Video files]. Retrieved from https://www.youtube.com/watch?v=u5aWcN5GJ68.
Annie E. Casey Foundation. (2017). 2017 Kids count data book: State trends in child well-being. Retrieved from http://www.aecf.org/m/resourcedoc/aecf-2017kidscountdatabook.pdf.
Darragh, J. J. & Hill, C. (2014). "The worst form of violence": Unpacking portrayals of poverty in young adult novels. In C. Hill (Ed.), *The critical merits of young adult literature.* New York: Routledge.

Dotson-Lewis, B. L. (2009, February 15). Speak your piece: Diane Sawyer in Eastern Kentucky. *The Daily Yonder*. Retrieved from https://www.dailyyonder.com/speak-your-piece-diane-sawyer-eastern-kentucky/2009/02/15/1933/.

Eichelberger, E. (2014). 10 poverty myths, busted. *Mother Jones*. Retrieved from https://www.motherjones.com/politics/2014/03/10-poverty-myths-busted/.

Family and Consumer Sciences. (n.d.). Living in poverty lesson. Retrieved from https://www.familyconsumersciences.com/wp-content/uploads/Living-in-Poverty-Lesson.pdf.

Gorski, P. (2007). The question of class. *Teaching Tolerance, 31*. Retrieved from https://www.tolerance.org/magazine/spring-2007/the-question-of-class.

Gorski, P. (2008). The myth of the culture of poverty. *Educational Leadership, 65*(7), 32–36. Retrieved from http://www.ascd.org/publications/educationalleadership/apr08/vol65/num07/The-Myth-of-the-Culture-of-Poverty.aspx.

Hill, C. & Darragh, J. J. (2017). Is poverty the result of poor decisions?: What young adult literature contributes to the conversation. In J. A. Hayn, J. S. Kaplan, & K. R. Clemmons (Eds.), *Teaching young adult literature today* (pp. 85–99). Lanham, MD: Rowman & Littlefield.

McMillan, T. (2017, July 8). What do we think poverty looks like? *New York Times*. Retrieved from https://www.nytimes.com/2017/07/08/opinion/sunday/poverty-snap-food-stamps-.html.

National Center for Children in Poverty (NCCP). (2018). Child poverty. Retrieved from http://www.nccp.org/topics/childpoverty.html.

Pimpare, S. (2018). Where are all the films about poor Americans? *The Guardian*. Retrieved from https://www.theguardian.com/commentisfree/2018/mar/05/film-poverty-america-policy-oscars.

Porter, E. (2015, October 20). The myth of welfare's corrupting influence on the poor. *New York Times*. Retrieved from https://www.nytimes.com/2015/10/21/business/the-myth-of-welfares-corrupting-influence-on-the-poor.html.

SPENT. (2011). Retrieved fromhttp://playspent.org.

Teaching Tolerance. (1991–2018). Issues of poverty. Retrieved from https://www.tolerance.org/classroom-resources/tolerance-lessons/issues-of-poverty.

US Department of Agriculture. (2018). Rural poverty & well-being. Retrieved from https://www.ers.usda.gov/topics/rural-economy-population/rural-poverty-well-being.

Zentner, J. (2016). *The serpent king.* New York: Penguin Random House.

9

POLICE BRUTALITY

Racial tensions in the United States, specifically between Black and White individuals, are not new. Since the civil rights movements in the 1960s, when police assaulted African American protesters across the South; through the recorded and released beating of Rodney King in 1991 by Los Angeles officers; to debates over affirmative action policies in college admissions in the 2000s, this country has a history of violence and backlash related to race. And yet, in 2012, the problem drew unprecedented national attention through the shooting of Trayvon Martin and the acquittal of George Zimmerman. Unfortunately, attacks such as Martin's have continued into the last decade, and names such as Sandra Bland, Eric Garner, and Michael Brown have become familiar as victims of police crimes are recognized nationally and a pattern of killing persists.

A manifestation of racism in society, police brutality involves the unnecessary and unwarranted use of force generally by White officers on Black bodies. Using their authority, White officers unlawfully indict, detain, or punish individuals, "many of them unarmed. . . . Such excessive force by police is particularly disturbing given its disproportionate impact on people of color" (ACLU, 2018, para. 1). Often, these officers are not charged with wrongdoing, citing self-defense or claiming to have been performing their duties (Bellafante, 2014). This rightfully leads to outrage and protests by concerned citizens, as families are left without their loved ones and justice is not served.

While personal and implicit biases are often linked to such cases, showing that officers are given to racist tendencies, the issue is much larger than one individual (Holmes & Smith, 2008). The web of racism is intricate and can be difficult for secondary students to understand because racism is constructed as either individual acts of discrimination and, relatedly, a thing of the past. It is easier to say "a cop is racist" because he beat up a young Black man than to acknowledge there is a structure in the United States that conditions individuals toward such behavior and then does nothing to disrupt it.

Racism is thus a systemic issue, meaning it is much larger than one person, although people certainly uphold and perpetuate it both knowingly and unknowingly (Sensoy & DiAngelo, 2012). It is woven into the fabric of daily life so tightly that it can be difficult to untangle. For example, studies of resume screenings have shown that individuals with ethnic minority identifiers, meaning their names "sound" to belong to a race or ethnicity other than White, are more likely to be rejected from the application process than ethnic majority (White) identifiers (Derous & Ryan, 2012). Access to jobs, then, can be affected by race.

Racism works alongside White privilege, a system in which individuals with lighter colored skin are afforded unearned benefits, such as obtaining financial breaks and loans, being reflected consistently in classroom curriculum, and being assumed as the "norm" against which those who are *not* are judged and othered. Kendall (2002) writes, "One of the primary privileges is that of having greater access to power and resources than people of color do; in other words, purely on the basis of our skin color doors are open to us that are not open to other people" (p. 1). Assumptions about people with light skin include their being honest, responsible, and safe. Thus, White privilege also simultaneously works through the oppression of people of color, about which the opposite assumptions are made—they are often portrayed (especially through the media) as unsafe, powerless, and less deserving of resources such as health care.

In this chapter, we focus on the novel *All American Boys* by Jason Reynolds and Brendan Kiely (2015) to help students work through the implications of racism and police brutality. Reading about youth who are similar in age will potentially help students discern how they are affected by racial relations in their own lives and to consider (and hopefully act on) the methods through which they can enact change to combat the negative effects of racial inequity.

ALL AMERICAN BOYS

All American Boys is a novel that reflects an incident of police brutality through the perspectives of two adolescent males, one Black (Rashad) and one White (Quinn). Told in alternating points of view, the story catalogs how Rashad is wrongly assaulted by a police officer, Paul, who mistakenly assumes that Rashad is stealing from a local convenience store. Paul's attack is ruthless and leaves Rashad with a broken nose, fractured ribs, and internal bleeding from torn blood vessels around his lungs.

Quinn, a classmate of Rashad's, accidentally stumbles upon the scene and watches from the shadows, horrified and astonished that Paul, a person he looked up to as an older brother, could commit such violence. As the novel progresses, Rashad is treated in the hospital for his wounds and is encouraged by his brother Spoony to confront the racist act of which he is a survivor. Raised by his former-police-officer traditional father who is "all about discipline and believed that if you work hard, good things happen to you no matter what" (Reynolds & Kiely, 2015, p. 51), Rashad learns more about his family and struggles to come to terms with institutional racism and its impact.

As the story progresses, Quinn learns to recognize his White privilege and to speak out for others. His best friend, Guzzo, is Paul's brother, who has served as a father figure to Quinn after Quinn's own father was killed in Afghanistan while serving in the US military. Being raised by a single mother, Quinn wrestles with defying close friends and family members to do what is right, recognizing that if he does not act against such forms of racism, the system will continue to thrive. In the end, all characters participate in a march to protest police brutality and perform a die-in, or laying on the ground to protest. They then read a list of real names to honor those who have suffered from such assault. The novel's conclusion, however, does not include any indication of what becomes of Paul, and thus readers are left in somewhat of a state of uncertainty regarding systemic racism and justice.

All American Boys is an especially valuable text because it simultaneously tackles White privilege and racial oppression, rather than focusing only on one issue or the other. It provides students multiple perspectives from which to examine the social problem and does so in ways that are thoughtful and prompt dialogue. Thus, we chose this book to delve into police brutality because of the way it represents the themes from readers' potential viewpoints and because it challenges and informs its audience.

TEACHING STRATEGIES

Before Reading

The context in which a teacher works will certainly influence the approach they should take with this novel. Often, students of color will be familiar with systemic discrimination and racism, having experienced it in their own lives. White students who may be less familiar with structural privilege will need an introduction to the concept. All students, however, could benefit from unpacking key terms. Thus, we suggest that teachers begin with basic vocabulary with which to discuss the topic of the book and the social problem it addresses, including terms such as *privilege, oppression, microaggressions, discrimination, prejudice, race,* and *socialization.* It will be key to note that:

> Oppression is different from prejudice and discrimination in that prejudice and discrimination describe dynamics that occur on the individual level and in which all individuals participate. In contrast, oppression occurs when one group's prejudice is *backed by historical, social and institutional power.* (Sensoy & DiAngelo, 2012, p. 39)

Students must understand that discrimination can happen against any one person by another, but oppression includes an element of power and works on a larger scale. In order to facilitate understandings, teachers could ask students to give examples from their own experiences or from events in society to demonstrate their understanding of each of the above terms (once definitions have been provided).

Other concepts for discussion include the use of *White, people of color, Black,* and *African American.* Students could read a few informational texts to more deeply consider these topics, such as *The Observer* (Mendez, 2016) article, "Should We Say Black or African American?" and Ta-Nehisi Coates's (2013) essay, "What We Mean When We Say 'Race Is a Social Construct.'" Discussion questions based on these two could include: *Why should people self-identify their race or ethnicity, rather than having someone label them? What does it mean to say race is socially constructed? How is race important in our society?*

Once students have a basis for engaging in conversation around these issues, teachers can move them into considering White privilege as a system. They might ask students to construct a list, similar to Peggy McIntosh's (1989), of the benefits and unearned advantages that White individuals experience in our society. McIntosh (1989) catalogues the everyday benefits she experiences, such as being able to find bandages that match her flesh or not being assumed to represent her entire race if she makes a mistake. Reading her list and updating it would be helpful, and students could complete this activity regardless of their own racial identity to denote the aspects of White privilege that permeate today's world. They could be encouraged to consider television, movies, and music, such as Macklemore, Ryan Lewis, and Jamila Woods's song, "White Privilege II," as well as everyday activities such as shopping and resources available in hotels and grocery stores. Teachers could assign these categories to groups of students so that they are looking collectively at our culture with a critical eye rather than only at their individual selves.

Beyond these sorts of individual privileges, however, it is key to help students discern the systemic nature of racial oppression. Applebaum (2010) warns against merely stopping at "white privilege pedagogy" (p. 29) because "students often walk away from reading McIntosh's article thinking that all there is to being anti-racist is 'taking off the knapsack' without acknowledging that privilege is often ascribed even when one is not aware of it and even when one refuses it" (p. 31). Instead, she advocates for utilizing "white complicity pedagogy" (p. 179), which focuses on the ways that the dominant group maintains their status and encourages individuals to discern their part in upholding the status quo.

In order to illustrate this for students, teachers can ask students to practice skills of critical literacy and to examine instances in which ignorance or complicity exists, both historic and current, and to ask them to imagine how people could act differently in that situation. For instance, they might examine the case of Silent Sam, the statue of a confederate soldier at the University of North Carolina at Chapel Hill that was torn down by protestors and set off a firestorm of debate. Teachers might ask students, upon learning about Silent Sam and the issues surrounding his existence on campus: *Who were the protestors? Who were the bystanders? Who had privilege in this situation, and how could they have used those privileges productively, for the safety and betterment of students of color on this campus?*

Helping students understand that racism is everyone's issue is vital. As Jill tells Quinn in the novel, "But everyone's seen it, Quinn. It's *all our* problem. But what *is* the problem?" (p. 182). Facilitating students' ability to name the problem and address it are key classroom goals for the study of this text. Teaching Tolerance (2017) has some great resources for helping teachers prepare to talk with students about race and for engaging in those difficult conversations, such as a self-evaluation for teachers to assess their own comfort levels talking about race and strategies for facilitating related discussions with youths.

During Reading

As students read the novel, they will likely identify with one or the other of the protagonists—Quinn or Rashad. Teachers could select one point in the book, such as after the incident of brutality or when tensions rise on the basketball team, and ask students to compose a diary entry, tweet, or Facebook post, as if they were one of the two characters. Or, they could write a letter to the protagonist with which they most identify (Quinn or Rashad) and explain the connections they experience. These text-to-self-connections (Rosenblatt, 1938) are key for honoring all students' voices in the classroom and highlighting the different ways that they will relate to the text. They might choose to share these with the class as a way of explaining their own relationship with race in their context.

Students could also be encouraged to empathize with the difficult decisions each of the protagonists makes in the story as they develop their understandings of race and society. At first, Rashad does not wish to become the face of a movement. He says, "I gotta admit, there was a part of me that, even though I felt abused, wanted to tell him [Spoony] to let it go. To just let me heal, let me leave the hospital, let me go to court, let me do whatever stupid community service they wanted me to do, and let me go back to normal" (p. 59). Teachers can ask students to consider: *Why would Rashad not want to be on the news? Why would he admit to doing something he didn't do and perform community service? Why might Rashad not want to be the face of a protest? What do you think eventually makes him embrace the role he does?*

At the same time, Quinn struggles to understand his White privilege and worries about his responsibility in reporting what he has seen during the incident. He realizes, "If I wanted to, I could walk away and not think about Rashad, in a way that . . . any of the guys at school who were not white could not . . . my shield was white. . . . It wasn't only that I could walk away—I already *had* walked away" (p. 180). Realizing, as mentioned above with the danger of the knapsack metaphor from McIntosh's work, that he cannot take off his skin color but instead that he has unearned advantages because of it, Quinn begins to embrace his responsibility. He avows, "And if I don't do something . . . if I just stay silent, it's just like saying it's not my problem" (p. 184). Teachers can ask students here: *Why is it difficult for Quinn to speak up and report what he saw to the police? What does Quinn sacrifice by making a report? Why does Quinn try to justify what happened to Rashad to his friends on the basketball team?*

Students could create digital stories about a time they had to speak up or take action to do what was right, or they could research key figures in history and share those stories with classmates. They could also note the similarities and differences between these individuals and Quinn or Rashad. Digital stories require research, writing, storyboarding, and a host of other technical elements that promote students' various literacies (Robin, 2008) and are engaging ways to share information.

Another aspect around which to cultivate students' critical literacies is through media representations related to race. In the novel, Rashad's brother Spoony releases a photo of Rashad in his ROTC uniform for the media, saying he wanted "to make sure we controlled as much of the narrative as possible," because if he had not he was certain the news reporters would have "dug all through the Internet for some picture of you looking crazy" (p. 94). In order to scaffold students' critical media literacies (Morrell, Dueñas, Garcia, & López, 2013), they could begin by examining movie posters that tell stories of youths, examining how the images differ based on the youths portrayed—inner city youths of color are often portrayed in dark colors with images that instill fear while White youths are depicted in bright colors and ways that promote a "party" storyline (Trier, 2005).

Teachers can then utilize resources provided by the Critical Media Project (2018a), which provide an overview of stereotypes in the media and contain clips with discussion questions. One that relates well to the discussion of *All American Boys* is the Pepsi advertisement (Critical Media Project, 2018b) that gained negative attention for its casual treatment of the #BlackLivesMatter movement. Teachers can then prompt students to consider the depiction of the protest in the advertisement, which they could then relate back to the march in the novel.

Finally, students could conduct character analyses of the major figures in the book. Many of the characters are dynamic in nature, such as Rashad's father, who shifts from a mentality of blaming Rashad to having a more sympathetic attitude toward Rashad's innocence. Most of the characters therefore undergo major transformations and exemplify internal growth. Students can trace this development through illustrations of each character's journey and/or symbolic images to represent the entities that become most important to each character. These will lead to how race is a defining aspect of each character's identity and development. For example, Quinn's whiteness is something he comes to recognize, question, and battle, and students could choose to represent that metaphorically in their artistic responses.

After Reading

The conclusion of the book does not offer a tidy culmination of its events. For some students, especially those who desire a happy ending, this can be difficult to process. Teachers could suggest that students compose and act out scenes they imagine would happen after where the book leaves off, either in the near or distant future. Students could write scripts and perform them for their classmates to illustrate the world they want to live in or to show where they hope the characters would be in the time to come.

The realistic nature of the ending, however, which portrays resistance but not necessarily justice for Rashad, shows the complex nature of the topics tackled in the book, and this ending is worth having students consider deeply. Students could therefore research the history of resistance, especially in movements such as the civil rights movement of the 1960s and the #BlackLivesMatter movement, and discuss the forms of resistance taken and the achievements for change such movements have secured.

As many critique classroom curricula for romanticizing the civil rights movements, it is important that students understand the historic oppression in which today's events are rooted rather than highlighting a few key figures and only praising them as heroes. Pitts (2017) offers guiding questions for this research, such as, "What distinguishes a rebellion from a riot? Whose murders are labeled genocide? What racial groups and tactics of resistance are praised over others?"

Once students have researched these histories, they can then draw connections to contemporary instances of police brutality and racism. In groups, they can investigate one case of police brutality and examine court documents, news articles, and firsthand narratives to construct their understanding of the instance and then share it with the class. As a whole class, they can trace patterns across these cases to again discern how the issue is systemic and broad reaching.

In order to further emphasize the institutionalized nature of racism, students could research national and local policies for training police, especially as related to implicit bias. They would first need to unpack the concept of implicit bias, which "refers to the attitudes or stereotypes that affect our understanding, actions, and decisions in an unconscious manner" and "are activated involuntarily and without an individual's awareness or intentional control" (Kirwan Institute, 2015, para. 1). Students can examine an Implicit Association Test themselves that assesses the test taker's own biases, and they could explore the Project Implicit (2011) website.

In the novel, Quinn states, "I don't think most people think they're racist," to which Jill later responds, "I think it's all racism" (Reynolds & Kiely, 2015, p. 184). The notion of implicit bias will help students discern that while individuals may not consider themselves racist because they do not commit individual acts of discrimination openly or knowingly, social conditioning leads many to harbor negative associations with people of different races. This can be connected to Rashad's dad in the book, who mistakenly assumes a Black adolescent male is culpable in a fight with a White male. These biases are deeply embedded in our culture and can infiltrate the psyche of all members.

IDEAS FOR SOCIAL ACTION

From the research conducted after reading, students can then move into action. Students might decide to organize their own resistance movements, protesting police brutality at large, or they could choose a more local (even school) issue dealing with racism about which to raise awareness and work to remedy. For instance, students might wish to address microaggressions, or "brief and commonplace daily verbal, behavioral, or environmental indignities, whether intentional or unintentional, that communicate hostile, derogatory, or negative racial slights and insults toward people of color" (Sue et al., 2007, p. 271). These include comments such as, "'You [a Black person] are not like the rest of them. You're different,' 'If only there were more of them [Black people] like you [a Black person],' and 'I don't think of you [a Black person] as Black'" (Solórzano, Ceja, & Yosso, 2000, pp. 60–61).

In order to act for change surrounding microaggressions, students might design a poster campaign, sharing examples of microaggressions through social media and visibly throughout the halls of their school to encourage their peers to stop using damaging language. They could research common microaggressions and provide evidence of how these are psychologically destructive to the groups they target.

Students might also design a survey to implement at their school to determine what areas of racial inequity are most prevalent and need to be addressed, and they could analyze the results and present their findings to school administrators, board members, and district representatives and provide recommendations for addressing the concerns they collected.

From their research on resistance, students might also write and perform their own protest songs or poems at an open-mic night hosted at the school. This would require research on popular songs and poems of resistance from the past and the movements they supported, such as Curtis Mayfield's "People Get Ready," Sam Cooke's "A Change Is Gonna Come," or Gil Scott Heron's "The Revolution Will Not Be Televised." Students might attempt to emulate these and relate them to their present concerns. They might also wish to examine current songs, such as Childish Gambino's "This Is America," which rocked the popular music scene in 2018 for its graphic presentation of injustice in the country. Students could consider why such songs receive national attention and how they reflect those affected as well as the public conversation about topics such as racism and police brutality.

Since police brutality is an issue that affects the entire community, students could organize a community meeting to discuss the issue and generate solutions. They might consider a public reading group in which parents, stakeholders, and community members are invited to read and discuss the book with the students (Boyd & Darragh, 2019). Engaging in intergenerational dialogue about racism could deepen understandings as well as develop empathy among all participants.

Students might also wish to broaden their study of police brutality and race to examine how other minoritized groups, such as Latinx and Native American populations, are similarly targeted. They could research specific instances, such as police assault at Standing Rock or even at the US border with Mexico, extending their understandings of how racialized groups are mistreated and are often the recipients of violence.

Finally, from their work on police training and implicit bias, students could create a document compiling suggestions for officer preparation and continued education. They might include articles, documentaries, and personal narratives they located and think are relevant. The key here is that their recommendations are research based but are balanced with their own creative ideas for what could make a more just world for all. Enacting and offering solutions to police brutality will help students see that this is a social problem that can and should be addressed.

SUPPLEMENTAL RESOURCES

Canonical Companions

To Kill a Mockingbird by Harper Lee
Invisible Man by Ralph Ellison
Native Son by Richard Wright

Connected Young Adult Literature

How It Went Down by Kekla Magoon
The Hate U Give by Angie Thomas
When I Was the Greatest by Jason Reynolds
March by John Lewis, Andrew Aydin, and Nate Powell

Connected Music

"This Is America" by Childish Gambino

"People Get Ready" by Curtis Mayfield

"A Change Is Gonna Come" by Sam Cooke

"The Revolution Will Not Be Televised" by Gil Scott-Heron

"White Privilege II" by Macklemore and Ryan Lewis feat. Jamila
Woods

REFERENCES

American Civil Liberties Union (ACLU). (2018). Police excessive force. Retrieved from https:/
/www.aclu.org/issues/criminal-law-reform/reforming-police-practices/police-excessive-
force.

Applebaum, B. (2010). *Being White, being good: White complicity, White moral responsibility,
and social justice pedagogy.* Lanham, MD: Lexington Books.

Bellafante, G. (2014, December 4). Police violence seems to result in no punishment. *New York
Times.* Retrieved from https://www.nytimes.com/2014/12/07/nyregion/police-violence-
seems-to-result-in-no-punishment.html.

Boyd, A. S. & Darragh, J. J. (2019). Complicating censorship: Reading *All American Boys* with
parents of young adults. *English Education, 51*(3), 229–260.

Coates, T.-N. (2013, May 15). What we mean when we say "race is a social construct." *The
Atlantic.* Retrieved from https://www.theatlantic.com/national/archive/2013/05/what-we-
mean-when-we-say-race-is-a-social-construct/275872/.

Critical Media Project. (2018a). Pepsi protest ad (Kendall Jenner). Retrieved from http://
criticalmediaproject.org/2088-2/.

Critical Media Project. (2018b). Topic overview: Race and ethnicity. Retrieved from http://
criticalmediaproject.org/wp-content/uploads/2018/03/Race-and-Ethnicity-Topic.pdf.

Derous, E. & Ryan, A. M. (2012). Documenting the adverse impact of résumé screening:
Degree of ethnic identification matters. *International Journal of Selection and Assessment,
20*(4), 464–474.

Holmes, M. D. & Smith, B. W. (2008). *Race and police brutality: Roots of an urban dilemma.*
New York: State University of New York Press.

Kendall, F. E. (2002). Understanding white privilege. Retrieved from https://www.cpt.org/files/
Undoing%20Racism%20-%20Understanding%20White%20Privilege%20-%20Kendall.
pdf.

Kirwan Institute for the Study of Race and Ethnicity. (2015). Understanding implicit bias.
Retrieved from http://kirwaninstitute.osu.edu/research/understanding-implicit-bias/.

McIntosh, P. (1989). White privilege: Unpacking the invisible knapsack. *Peace and Freedom
Magazine,* 10–12. Retrieved from https://www.deanza.edu/faculty/lewisjulie/White%
20Priviledge%20Unpacking%20the%20Invisible%20Knapsack.pdf.

Mendez, M. (2016, October 14). Should we say Black or African American? *The Observer.*
Retrieved from http://www.fordhamobserver.com/should-we-say-black-or-african-americ
an/.

Morrell, E., Dueñas, R., Garcia, V., & López, J. (2013). *Critical media pedagogy: Teaching for
achievement in city schools.* New York: Teachers College.

Pitts, J. (2017). Bringing black lives matter into the classroom part II. *Teaching Tolerance, 56.*
Retrieved from https://www.tolerance.org/magazine/summer-2017/bringing-black-lives-
matter-into-the-classroom-part-ii.

Project Implicit. (2011). Retrieved from https://implicit.harvard.edu/implicit/.

Reynolds, J. & Kiely, B. (2015). *All American boys.* New York: Simon & Schuster.

Robin, B. R. (2008). Digital storytelling: A powerful technology tool for the 21st century classroom. *Theory into Practice, 47*, 220–228.

Rosenblatt, L. M. (1938/1995). *Literature as exploration.* New York: The Modern Language Association of America.

Sensoy, Ö. & DiAngelo, R. (2012). *Is everyone really equal? An introduction to key concepts in social justice education.* New York: Teachers College Press; Routledge.

Solórzano, D., Ceja, M., & Yosso, T. (2000). Critical race theory, racial microaggressions, and campus racial climate: The experiences of African American college students. *Journal of Negro Education, 69*(1/2), 60–73.

Sue, D. W., Capodilupo, C. M., Torino, G. C., Bucceri, J. M., Holder, A. M. B., Nadal, K. L., & Esquilin, M. (2007). Racial microgressions in everyday life. *American Psychologist, 62*(4), 271–286.

Teaching Tolerance. (2017). Let's talk. Retrieved from https://www.tolerance.org/sites/default/files/2017-09/TT-Lets%20Talk-2017%20Final.pdf.

Trier, J. (2005). "Sordid fantasies": Reading popular "inner-city" school films as racialized texts with pre-service teachers. *Race Ethnicity and Education, 8*(2), 171–189.

10

IMMIGRATION REFORM

Dating back to the English-speaking Protestant Christians of the seventeenth century, what is now the United States of America has always been a country of immigrants. The "American Dream," the idea that, upon living in the United States, if one has a strong work ethic success will follow, has long been a motivation for those who are struggling in their own country to leave and start anew. However, for a country largely developed by immigrants, the United States also has a controversial history of denying specific groups the chance to pursue their own "American Dream."

Creating formal, legal barriers for immigrants can be traced back to 1790 with the Naturalization Act, which "excluded non-white people from eligibility to naturalize" (Cohn, 2015, para. 2). Later, in 1921 and 1924, laws were passed limiting immigration, "capping total annual immigration and imposing numerical quotas based on immigrant nationality that favored northern and western European countries" (Cohn, 2015, para. 5).

And while in 1952 "race was formally removed as grounds for exclusion" of being welcomed into the United States, in 1965 the Immigration and Nationality Act "created a new system favoring family reunification and skilled immigrants, rather than country quotas. The law also imposed the first limits on immigration from the Western Hemisphere. Before then, Latin Americans had been allowed to enter the U.S. without many restrictions" (Cohn, 2015, para. 7).

More recently, in January 2017, President Trump signed two executive orders that further limited immigration opportunities. Executive Order 13,767 paved the way for massive deporting of undocumented residents, adding detention facilities for undocumented immigrants, and discontinuing due process for asylum seekers (Executive Order No. 13,767, 2017), and Executive Order 13,769 created a travel ban to prevent arrivals to the United States of those departing from seven Muslim-majority countries (Executive Order No. 13,769, 2017).

Clearly, the United States has a long and complicated history regarding immigration, and it is likely that students have heard conflicting information from multiple sources—the nation's leaders, the media, and even their own family members and friends. In order to help students to better understand the complexity of immigration in the United States, we suggest a unit of study centered on the YA nonfiction text *Enrique's Journey: The True Story of a Boy Determined to Reunite with His Mother.*

ENRIQUE'S JOURNEY

Sonia Nazario's (2013) Pulitzer Prize–winning *Enrique's Journey: The True Story of a Boy Determined to Reunite with His Mother* follows sixteen-year-old Enrique who, over the course of many months, travels from Honduras to the United States in order to reunite with his mother. While there are two versions of this book, we recommend the Young Adult adaptation due to its length and because some of the more graphic descriptions are adapted to make it more accessible for younger readers.

Enrique's mother left Honduras for the United States when he was five years old, in search of work and a better life for both herself and her children. Heartbroken, Enrique does not fully understand, feels his mother abandoned him, and begins to use drugs. This results in tumultuous relationships with his remaining family in Honduras as well as his girlfriend, María Isabel. He thus sets out to locate his mother in the United States and to reestablish their mother-son bond. Enrique leaves behind María Isabel, who is pregnant, to find his mother, and, like her, a better life for himself and his burgeoning family.

Readers live vicariously through Enrique, traveling upon the top of trains, across waters, and by land as he faces violence, starvation, brutality, and deportation. Enrique's mother eventually pays a smuggler to bring him into the country, but all does not end well when the two are reunited. They are forced to deal with years of separation, and Enrique, again, turns to drugs. Eventually he is able to bring his wife and daughter to the United States, but their lives continue to be challenging. Enrique's troubles are not only the result of his personal and family situations but also because Nazario's documentation of his story places him in danger in both the United States and his home country of Honduras.

This nonfiction text encourages readers to consider why people choose to leave their country, despite the great risks involved, as well as both the corruption and kindness of strangers. We chose *Enrique's Journey* for the focus of this chapter on immigration not only because it offers one teen's true immigration story, but also because the author raises many pertinent questions regarding the positive and negative impacts of immigration in the United States that have remained unchanged over the years.

TEACHING STRATEGIES

Before Reading

The Teaching Tolerance website offers a variety of lesson plan ideas that can easily be implemented as an introduction to a unit of study on immigration. For example, one provided lesson, titled "Immigration Myths," focuses "on facing some common misconceptions about immigrants as a group. By connecting stereotypes to myths and then dispelling those myths, students will confront the lies that are the foundation of bigotry toward immigrants" (1991–2018, para. 4).

For this activity, in order to establish a baseline of what students already know and believe, teachers write commonly believed misperceptions about immigration (e.g., *"Undocumented immigrants don't pay taxes and burden the national economy"*; *"Immigrants take good jobs from U.S. citizens"* [Teaching Tolerance, 1991–2018, para. 6]) on poster paper around the room. Students use a carousel approach, circulating to each paper, reading the myth, discussing it, and then writing a response to some posed questions such as: *Where do you think this myth comes from? Who benefits from this myth? Why is this myth untrue?* (Teaching Tolerance, 1991–2018, para. 6).

Students circulate to each paper, reading all that is written and adding their own responses. When they have completed the carousel, they can read an article provided on the website, "Ten Myths about Immigration," and as a whole class discuss whether or not they have heard the myths presented, what they have learned, and how they might be able to respectfully broach this topic to change misperceptions/misinformation if they hear people spreading information regarding immigrants that is not true (Teaching Tolerance, 1991–2018).

Teachers might want to first have students privately write about the myths—what they think about them, where they heard them, their personal experiences with them—before telling students that they are, indeed, myths. In all cases, teachers will need to be sensitive both to students who may be immigrants or from immigrant families and students who have family members who spread anti-immigrant sentiments, explicitly letting students know that all students are valued and should feel safe to share their thoughts and experiences.

PBS also offers a series of lesson plans regarding immigration that might be useful for teachers to introduce the topic of immigration. Connected to their series *New Americans*, students can watch videos that share various immigration stories, take quizzes, and do related activities like analyzing primary source documents and conducting their own oral history projects through audio and/or video recording the immigration stories of people they know (PBS, 2017). Teachers might also invite a guest speaker in who wants to share their own immigration story with the class. Students can then identify what they learned about the immigration experience presented as well as any misconceptions the shared stories addressed.

During Reading

As students read the book, they can consider what they would do if they found themselves in a similar situation as Enrique and/or Lourdes. Teachers can elicit critical thinking, text-to-self-connections, and the use of textual evidence to support claims as they pose questions like: *Why did Lourdes leave Honduras? Did she have other options? Why might she not have felt she had a choice? By leaving, what have she and her children lost and gained?*

In the Prologue, author Sonia Nazario poses questions that are also appropriate for students to consider verbally or in writing, individually, with a partner, or in a small group. She writes:

> I was struck by the choice mothers face when they leave their children. How do they make such an impossible decision? What would I do if I were in their shoes? Would I come to the United States, make much more money, and ensure that my children back home could eat and study past the third grade? Or would I stay with my children, even though they would grow up in miserable poverty? (p. 4)

Nazario continues by explaining some of her motivation for writing the book:

> In much of the United States, legitimate concerns about immigration and anti-immigrant measures have had a severe side effect: immigrants have been dehumanized and demonized. Perhaps, I thought, if I provided an in-depth look at one immigrant—his strengths, his courage, his flaws—his humanity might help shed light on what too often has been a black-and-white discussion. (p. 6)

As students are reading the book, they can track these identified characteristics of Enrique (strengths, courage, flaws, humanity), citing specific examples in a teacher-created table or chart. This can be done for other people mentioned in the book as well, such as Lourdes and María. Upon completing the book, students can refer to the chart, analyzing it for patterns and drawing conclusions about what this text says about humans in general, and immigrants in particular. They can compare these conclusions to what they see and hear regarding immigrants in the media, in their communities, and in their homes.

While reading the book and in order to more fully understand some of the barriers in becoming "documented" in the United States, teachers can utilize the Teacher Vision website (2000–2018), and have students take a quiz of questions that are commonly on a US citizenship test to see how they would perform. After taking the quiz, students can discuss the barriers immigrants like Lourdes and Enrique would face in taking the citizenship test.

The can also analyze the format, instructions, and the questions of the citizenship test. Students can identify what they perceive are the strengths and weaknesses of a test like this. Then, in groups, they might contemplate if they think the test in general and/or the questions in particular should be changed, and, if so, how and why?

Students might also be interested in analyzing songs that are written about the immigrant experience. In addition to those cited below, a quick internet search of the word *immigrant song* will reveal numerous titles, such as "The New Immigration Law" by Cocoa Tea, "Immigration Man" by Crosby and Nash, and "Immigrant Song" by Led Zeppelin.

Students can analyze lyrics of songs from different time periods, tracking recurring words that emerge, and from those, create their own art work, be it a Found Poem (Facing History, 2018), a collage, a bumper sticker, or other creation of their choice. Students can write their own songs or poems about Enrique's experiences or a scene in the book, or choose songs they feel best portray the mood, tone, and themes of this text.

After Reading

There are numerous resources online, including videos, lesson plans, and photos connected to this book, as it has been used widely in secondary and university classrooms across the country. As Sonia Nazario does much public speaking, it is easy to find interviews with her discussing the book and the immigration crisis. For example, an interview sponsored by Long Beach Library (2014) offers information about Nazario's inspiration for this research/book project. After watching this or a similar interview, students can brainstorm what questions they would like to ask the author if given the opportunity.

In the Long Beach interview, for example, Nazario shares that she looked for stories with universal themes, so she tried to tell that story through one boy—Enrique. Teachers might guide students to the "My Immigration Story" website (n.d.) to read other immigration stories, and perhaps add their own if they have a story to tell and choose to do so. They might also consider Nazario's role in telling the story: *How would the story be different if Enrique told it? If Lourdes told it? What does Nazario add to and take away from the story by telling it for Enrique?*

There is a website specifically for the book *Enrique's Journey* (2017). On it, teachers can find videos, photos, updates on the family, and links to a variety of lesson plans, such as the *New York Times*' learning blog that provides an activity that pairs *Enrique's Journey* with a *Times* article and slideshow and provides activities and discussion questions (Brown & Schulten, 2013).

Nazario mentions a variety of groups, nonprofits, and government agencies throughout the text that help Enrique and other immigrants, such as Grupos Beta; Office of Refugee Resettlement within the US Department of Health and Human Services; UNICEF; International Organization for Migration; and Kids in Need of Defense. Students can choose one of these to research, or search for other, local supports for immigrants, sharing the information gained in a written, oral, or multimedia presentation and comparing what they discover about these groups with the depictions of them in the text.

While *Enrique's Journey* focuses on more contemporary immigration issues and people from Central America, the book offers the opportunity to consider immigration trends, challenges, and successes of the past. From the Chinese Exclusion Act of 1882, to the Immigration Act of 1924 (also called the Johnson-Reed Act), which was the first law regarding setting quotas on the number of immigrants who could enter the United States from certain countries, students can research the history of immigration in this country, identifying patterns and trends and trying to determine why, at certain points in time, restrictions on immigration are put into place.

In a similar comparison activity, teachers can guide students through analyzing primary source documents regarding treatment of immigrants. For example, students can analyze FDR's Executive Order 9,066, which called for the forced evacuation and incarceration of 110,000 Japanese Americans, and President Trump's Executive Order 13,769 making comparisons between the two.

Specifically, students can exercise their critical literacies and study the language used in each order, identifying how word choice can be used to elicit emotional responses. For example, specific words and phrases used in these orders, like *protecting, security, terrorist,* and *espionage,* have obvious intentions of making the American public feel a certain way regarding the necessity of the orders. This primary source activity would allow students the opportunity to not only analyze documents but also rhetoric.

The documentary *Forgotten Ellis Island* (Conway, 2008) is about the hospital on Ellis Island where many immigrants stayed in order to make sure they had a clean bill of health before being admitted into the United

States. Students might be interested in researching medical practices of the past, such as how mental illness was "diagnosed" and the creation of public health. They can compare public health and medical practices, policies, and procedures used in the Ellis Island Hospital with those of today, identifying ways in which practices have improved over the years as well as challenges this and other countries are still facing in regard to health care (see also chapter 2, Global Poverty, and chapter 3, Mental Health).

IDEAS FOR SOCIAL ACTION

When considering projects for social action, students might want to model their work after Youth Breaking Borders (YBB). This leadership program for children and teens who are immigrants and refugees offers opportunities for "immigrant youth (to) produce critical media that aims to challenge dominant oppressive narratives about immigrants. The films have been used as educational tools to challenge Islamophobia, anti-blackness and to uplift the particular struggles of young immigrants of mixed status" (Global Action Project, n.d., para. 1).

Students might want to watch some of these films and then create their own. Teachers can help students to organize a film festival in their school or in the community, where students can premier their work. They can accept donations at the door that can be donated to local organizations that support immigrants in the community.

Connected to film, the documentary *Children of the Internment: German Families in US Camps* (Crump & Wagner, 2013) uses firsthand accounts to share what it was like for Germans, Italians, and Japanese Americans who were forced into internment camps during World War II. In the film, one interviewee, who was interned as a child, says that information about the internment camps, especially the sections of the camps for people with German and Italian ties, could not be found in the textbooks he or his children used in school.

Students can investigate whether this is still true by analyzing social studies textbooks for various grade levels for representation of voices and experiences. They can identify whose story is told and whose voice is silenced. If they feel a particular group has been left out of the curriculum, they might want to research options of books and resources that are inclusive, and propose those resources be considered for implementation into the curriculum at a faculty or school board meeting.

Students might also be interested in interviewing an immigration lawyer, and, if possible, attend an immigration trial. They can create a pamphlet for immigrants outlining their rights, resources, and contact information of supports that might be helpful to them if they are struggling. The pamphlets can be in multiple languages and with many clear visuals to help aid understanding for those for whom English is not their primary language (see chapter 6, Refugee Crisis).

In conducting their own primary research, students can collect immigration stories from people in their community. Using interview techniques, they can audio or video record the stories shared, edit and compile them as appropriate, and from those create a film or literary magazine that can be distributed or made available at the local library, senior center, doctors' offices, and/or online.

Students can also analyze their own school, as well as the primary schools in their district. Using what they have learned about feelings of isolation that immigrants often experience, students can determine whether or not the schools are welcoming of *all* students, and, if so, in what ways? They can identify ways in which the buildings and classrooms can be more welcoming (e.g., signs in multiple languages, art work and bulletin boards representing a variety of voices), and then make a plan for how they can support such inclusivity efforts.

Most everyone has a strong connection with someone who is an immigrant, be it their great-grandparents, neighbors, or friends. A critical look at immigration in the United States, from the past to current practices, can hopefully help students to understand the complexity of this issue and inspire them to focus on building bridges with those who come to the United States seeking their own American Dream.

SUPPLEMENTAL RESOURCES

Canonical Companions

House on Mango Street by Sandra Cisneros
The Jungle by Upton Sinclair

Farewell to Manzanar by Jeanne Wakatsuki Houston and James D. Houston

Connected Young Adult Literature

American Born Chinese by Gene Luen Yang
The Sun Is Also a Star by Nicola Yoon
American Street by Ibi Zoboi
Uprising by Margaret Peterson Haddix

Connected Music

"Clandestino" by Manu Chao
"The New Immigration Law" by Cocoa Tea
"Immigration Man" by Crosby and Nash
"Immigrant Song" by Led Zeppelin
"Migra" by Santana

REFERENCES

Brown, A. C., & Schulten, K. (2013, October 17). Text to text: *Enrique's journey* and "In trek north, first lure is Mexico's other line." *The Learning Network: Teaching and Learning with the New York Times.* Retrieved from https://learning.blogs.nytimes.com/2013/10/17/text-to-text-enriques-journey-and-in-trek-north-first-lure-is-mexicos-other-line/.

Cohn, D. (2015). How U.S. immigration laws and rules have changed through history. Pew Research Center. Retrieved from http://www.pewresearch.org/fact-tank/2015/09/30/how-u-s-immigration-laws-and-rules-have-changed-through-history/.

Conway, L. (Director). (2008). *Forgotten Ellis Island.* [Documentary]. United States: Boston Film & Video Productions.

Crump, J. & Wagner, K. (2013). *Children of the internment: German families in US camps.* [Documentary]. United States: Dancing Spirit Productions.

Enrique's Journey. (2017). Retrieved from http://enriquesjourney.com.

Exec. Order No. 9066, C.F.R. 42-1563 (1942).

Exec. Order No. 13,767, 3 C.F.R. 8793-8797 (2017).

Exec. Order No. 13,769, 3 C.F.R. 8977-8982 (2017).

Facing History and Ourselves. (2018). Found poems. Retrieved from https://www.facinghistory.org/resource-library/teaching-strategies/found-poems.

Global Action Project. (n.d.). Youth breaking borders. Retrieved from https://www.global-action.org/youth-breaking-borders.

Long Beach Public Library. (2014). Sonia Nazario: *Enrique's journey* interview. Retrieved from https://www.youtube.com/watch?v=wV4nkU0Fsxk.

My Immigration Story. (n.d.). Retrieved from https://myimmigrationstory.com/.

Nazario, S. (2013). *Enrique's journey: The true story of a boy determined to reunite with his mother.* [Adapted for young people]. New York: Random House.

PBS. (2017). The new Americans: For educators. Retrieved from http://www.pbs.org/independentlens/newamericans/foreducators_index.html.

TeacherVision. (2000–2018). Citizenship test 1. Retrieved from https://www.teachervision.com/citizenship/citizenship-test-i.

Teaching Tolerance. (1991–2018). Immigration myths. Retrieved from https://www.tolerance.org/classroom-resources/tolerance-lessons/immigration-myths.

11

SEXUAL ORIENTATIONS AND STIGMAS

Although sexuality in itself is not a social problem, different forms of attraction often endure social stigmas. We live in a heteronormative and heterosexist culture, one in which the taken-for-granted norms of romantic relationships occur between a man and a woman and monogamy is universally expected. While same-sex marriage has become legally sanctioned in the United States and gains have been made to lessen intolerance, there remain many parts of our country in which homophobic slurs, bigotry, and harassment persist. Furthermore, the potential of legal setbacks continues to threaten same-sex couples in the United States.

For example, in 2018, the Trump administration issued a decision to "no longer provide visas for same-sex domestic partners of foreign diplomats and U.N. officials serving in the U.S." (Finnegan, 2018). This decision ignores the challenges that exist for those living in countries where same-sex marriage is not legal and especially those in which same-sex orientations are criminalized. Also, under the Trump administration, the Department of Health and Human Services' Office of Civil Rights approved sanctions to allow health care providers to discriminate based on religious or moral reasons (National Center for Transgender Equality, 2018).

In addition, several states have laws in place that allow child placement agencies to refuse LGBTQIA+ (lesbian, gay, bisexual, transgender, queer, intersex, asexual, and those that do not ascribe to one of those categories) families (Pieklo, 2018). Policies such as these perpetuate social inequity, supporting viewpoints that LGBTQIA+ individuals are somehow different and undeserving of the same rights as heterosexual people.

Beyond this broader scope of mistreatment for individuals who identify as LGBTQIA+, youth in these communities are particularly affected by lack of acceptance. The GLSEN National School Climate Survey (2018) reported that of those surveyed, "Over eight in 10 (85 percent) experienced verbal harassment based on a personal characteristic, and nearly two thirds (66 percent) experienced LGBTQ-related discrimination at school" (para. 4). In addition, the Human Rights Campaign (2018) reported "92% of LGBTQ youth say they hear negative messages about being LGBT. The top sources are school, the Internet and their peers" (para. 7). The educational context, then, is a crucial space for students regarding sexual orientation and support (or lack thereof).

Although GLSEN (2018) also reported that "school climates are slowly improving for LGBTQIA+ students" (para. 8) and there is "a decrease in homophobic remarks compared to all prior years," and this is affirming, the fact that any statistics exist that illustrate systemic negativity toward this sensitive population necessitates additional education and action. Students should not feel unsafe at school because of their sexual orientation, but rather the school environment should be a space to foster acceptance and understanding. As the middle and high school years are times when students are working through understanding their own sexual orientations and acknowledgment of others, it is crucial that teachers welcome conversations (rather than treat them as taboo) about sexual orientation into their curricula.

In this chapter, we focus on Jandy Nelson's novel *I'll Give You the Sun* (2014) as a way to facilitate conversations with students on issues related to same-sex relationships. We provide examples of how a text can offer opportunities for students to investigate different aspects of and themes surrounding sexuality from rights for individuals to social acceptance.

I'LL GIVE YOU THE SUN

Narrated by twins, brother and sister, *I'll Give You the Sun* traces the development of several relationships over time. Told in the alternating points of view of Noah and Jude who are highly competitive with one another, the story shifts back and forth between past and present as readers learn about the artistic talents of both protagonists, the death of their mother, and their love interests. As Noah befriends a neighbor, Brian, who attends boarding school during the academic year but stays nearby for the summer, Jude has her first sexual encounter with a local surfer who is several years older than her, a traumatic and confusing event to which she does not consent. After their mother's fatality, Jude and Noah each change dramatically—Noah becomes more outgoing and social while Jude cuts off her hair and retreats inward.

Throughout the story, readers uncover that Jude threw away Noah's application to a prestigious arts-based high school and thus only she was admitted, leaving Noah to feel that his art is inadequate and causing him to cease all related creative efforts and instead join the cross-country team and date a girl, Heather. Jude struggles with seeing the ghosts of her mother and grandmother, and she seeks to construct a piece of art from stone that she feels will redeem her and rid her of these apparitions. Her desire to learn this artistic medium leads her to Guillermo Garcia, a renowned yet disturbed artist who, it turns out, was having an affair with her mother prior to her death. Only Noah knew about the infidelity and attempted to conceal it after his mother's car accident, telling everyone involved instead that his mother planned to reconcile with his father.

Noah, meanwhile, falls in love with Brian, who wishes to keep his sexuality a secret, telling Noah that as a budding baseball star he fears he would lose his opportunity to be captain the following year. He tells Noah, referring to his teammates, "'these guys aren't'—he made finger quotes—'evolved'" (p. 279). Nonetheless, Noah outs Brian in a moment of jealousy and frustration, and Brian refuses to talk with Noah again until the end of the novel when the two reconnect months later. Noah gains admittance to the art school with Jude, and Jude's love interest, Oscar, delays their relationship because of their three-year age difference. Noah and Jude become separate individuals that can appreciate rather than depend on one another, and their father and Guillermo are able to work past the death of Noah and Jude's mother knowing the truth about her feelings about both of them.

We chose this book because it reflects the struggles of two adolescent boys coming to terms with their sexual orientations and the implications of their identities, which involve family and broader social acceptance by institutions such as sports. The book, however, does not solely focus on this issue. Rather, it shows how sexual orientation is only one aspect of a person's life among many others—a lesson that we feel is important for teens. Instead, the novel realistically depicts the complicated nature of life and its myriad trials.

TEACHING STRATEGIES

Before Reading

Prior to beginning this text with students, it is imperative that teachers both gauge their own and their students' understandings of individuals who identify as gay or lesbian. Teachers who are apprehensive or feel they need more knowledge to teach about these communities might consult The Safe Zone Project (n.d.), which offers free resources including curriculum for familiarizing people with information related to marginalized groups. Often local universities or community organizations will also offer ally training, which teachers could request and open to the entire school faculty as professional development. If not yet allies, teachers should work to become informed about what it means to be a supporter of populations who are gay, lesbian, or bisexual, and how they can enact their care in school environments. They should also seek to have their own questions answered before they teach about these topics so as to avoid misrepresentation.

Once teachers feel equipped to participate in discussions on LGBTQIA+ communities in their classrooms, they can begin to engage their students' dispositions as well. Undoubtedly, students' comfort, misconceptions, and personal experiences will vary by context, and thus the teacher will have to determine where to begin with regard to vocabulary and explanations. We suggest establishing a baseline list of key terms to utilize that include those in the LGBTQIA+ acronym as well as *sexual orientation, sex,* and *gender*. GLAAD (2018) hosts a thorough list of terms and definitions as well as a list of terms to avoid with explanations of why they are considered offensive.

These clarifications can help students recognize the power of language and ensure that they use the terms preferred by the populations themselves rather than external labels they have heard or seen elsewhere. During this conversation with youth, teachers should remind students (see chapter 4) that *sex* and *gender* are in fact separate entities and that sexual attraction can vary. The book *I'll Give You the Sun* surrounds issues of attraction, particularly between two adolescent males.

As further introduction and in order to help students discern how viewpoints have changed over time, students could research the histories of how LGBTQIA+ populations have been treated in the United States and create their own multimedia timelines. They might divide up according to specific groups (lesbian, gay, etc.) or choose to investigate the communities together. Specific laws and policies should be studied, including the medicalization of homosexuality in the American Psychiatric Association's diagnostic manual, the Stonewall Riots, Harvey Milk, the Hate Crimes Sentencing Enhancement Act, the Defense of Marriage Act, same-sex marriage laws, the repeal of "Don't Ask, Don't Tell" in the military, and the election of numerous officials to office who identify as LGBTQIA+.

Teachers could also assign these events to groups or pairs and then require students to teach their peers about them. They can prompt students to consider these various factors with questions such as: *How has society's acceptance of LGBTQIA+ individuals changed over time? What is evidence of that shift—what laws and policies exist (or have existed in the past) to either hinder or help these individuals? How and why have these groups experienced acts of discrimination?*

Finally, again depending on the maturity level of the students, teachers should establish ground rules for reading and discussion that not only emphasize the correct use of terms but that also respect diversity and treat the relationships in the story with sensitivity. There are a number of works commonly taught in the English classroom that include romantic relationships and physical interaction, including *Romeo and Juliet, The Odyssey,* and *Pride and Prejudice.* Teachers can share with students that they value all kinds of relationships, and this book is a reflection of that regard. As there will likely be students who identify as gay or lesbian in the class, it will be key for the teacher to ensure respect is maintained throughout the reading.

During Reading

As they are reading, students can visually chart the development of each character, filling in the details about each as they learn them. Since the story shifts in perspectives and time, this will help readers sort out the minutiae and deepen their comprehension. Students might even draw the plotline with specific delineations for flashbacks to aid in keeping up with what happens and when. Teachers can also engage students with the use of the "portrait" mechanism as a literary technique. These arise through-out each chapter in parenthesis, and students may even choose a few instances to draw themselves and to connect to the context of the chapter in which they occur. For example, during the party game in which Noah and Heather end up in a closet and kiss, the phrase "(SELF-PORTRAIT: Boy in a Blender)" (p. 134) appears. Students could draw what they envision Noah means here and discuss how it relates and why Noah would feel this way at this moment, when he is kissing a girl.

Also while they read, students can analyze the progression of Jude and Noah's relationship. The two are extremely close when the novel begins, and students will likely relate to the familial bonds between siblings. The teacher can complicate students' perspectives through an analysis of the competitive nature of the characters by asking: *What are the advantages and disadvantages of Noah and Jude's relationship? How do they con-nect differently with each parent? Is Jude too protective of Noah? Do they go "too far" in their competition with one another, and, if so, how?*

As the story unfolds, readers learn that there are many secrets and unknown entities among the characters. For example, although Noah and Jude's mother and father separate, the audience is not sure if their father knows about her affair; Jude does not tell Noah that she and Brian did not kiss in the closet during the game at the party until much later; it is unknown what Noah's mother actually told Guillermo before she died; and Noah's father believes Noah is dating Heather and is heterosexual.

Students might seize these opportunities to make predictions as they read and respond to any number of surfacing questions, such as: *What happened to Guillermo that made him stop taking students? Who took pictures of Jude's statues and sent them to the art school? What is the actual story of Noah and Jude's mother's death? Why does Noah change? Do Noah and Brian ever get back together/talk?*

Students could also compose imaginary conversations in the forms of letters or even text messages from one character to another (Noah to Dad; Jude to mom; mom to dad; etc.) at any point in the novel, to either explain something they have kept secret or to share with the readers what they think should have been said. This could help students fill in gaps in the story they deem worthy of attention.

Further engaging students' creative capacities and reflecting Jude's experience, students could create a piece of art, music, or poetry that communicates a message they are not able to express otherwise to an individual other than themselves. They could write an artist's statement in which they explain their work and draw specific textual connections to Jude's predicament in the novel, describing how their pieces express a specific message. As inspiration, they might listen to No Doubt's song "Just a Girl" and consider it a representation of Jude feeling ignored by the world, and especially her encounter with Zephyr.

Teachers can also prompt students to analyze the title of the text and the various ways the "sun" becomes a central metaphor in the novel. They can keep a running record of how "the sun" is used in the text and examine how it takes on meaning each time it manifests. For instance, in negotiating for his drawing of the mysterious Oscar, Jude tells Noah, "I'll give you the sun" (p. 74). This references the customary game the two have of playfully dividing the world between them, and Jude's offering of the sun illustrates just how attracted to Oscar she is, foreshadowing the future in which she meets and falls in love with the real Oscar.

In addition to Jude's relationship, Noah and Brian develop a connection over the course of the novel. It is initially unclear if theirs is a budding romance or simply a close friendship. To solicit students' consideration, teachers might ask students: *Are Brian and Noah friends or more than that? How do you know? How do we traditionally categorize relationships—what are the requirements for friendship and for romance? Do Brian and Noah meet those definitions?*

Once it has been established that Noah and Brian are in fact attracted to one another, Brian tells Noah, "Just don't worry, okay?" (p. 121). Although Brian does not elaborate, the reader is led to assume he means that he does in fact feel the same way about Noah that Noah feels about him. The two eventually share a kiss, but Brian tells Noah, "No one can know. . . . Ever" (p. 273). Nonetheless, on the next few pages Brian flirts with a girl, Courtney, and goes into a closet with Jude during a game at a party. This eventually sends Noah into a rage and leads him to verbally share Brian's sexuality with Courtney, screaming at the two of them on the street, "He's gay, Courtney! Brian Connelly is gay!" (p. 288).

There are a number of aspects of Noah and Brian's relationship to unpack. First, teachers can ask students to speculate what Brian means when tells Noah not to worry. Then, they can consider: *Why doesn't Brian want anyone to know about his sexuality? Why would he pretend to like Courtney? Why would Noah disclose Brian's sexuality to Courtney, and are his actions understandable? How could this scene have gone differently?*

Students might then read other coming-out stories (e.g., Bauer, 1994) and compare those experiences and stories with Brian's and Noah's. Students should consider how important it is for a person who identifies as LGBTQIA+ to identify themselves and control their own narrative, rather than have someone do this for them. Not only is this an issue of personal preference, but it is a safety one as well, as Brian had already experienced violence from his teammates and with Noah earlier in the novel. Students might also discuss how Brian and Noah uphold and defy traditional stereotypes of gay men and how each struggles to understand and define themselves—especially in light of others such as their parents and teammates.

The parents' reactions are also an important part of this story to examine. Noah's mother walks in on a sexual scene between the two boys, after which Noah attempts to deny what she saw. She tells Noah, "'Listen to me. It takes a lot of courage to be true to yourself, true to your heart" (p. 281). Noah mistakenly thinks his mother is upset at having a gay son and fears his father's reaction. Teachers can challenge students' critical reflection on this topic by asking: *Why would Noah lie to his mother about his sexuality? What are Noah's father's expectations of him as a boy? Do you think he will be upset when he learns of Noah's sexuality?*

In terms of sexual encounters, there are also additional episodes in the novel that should be discussed. In particular, Jude is assaulted by Zephyr, a man years older than her with whom she was in a developing relationship. Although he tells her *"You can totally say no,"* Jude recounts "it seemed like he meant the opposite" (p. 46). Jude shares details throughout the remainder of the novel about how she and her mother conflicted about her choice of clothing and Noah details her flirtatious personality.

It is imperative that teachers devote attention to the implications of Jude's mother's and Noah's words so as to avoid victim blaming and to emphasize that Jude did not in fact give consent and that Zephyr was much older than Jude, she "in eighth grade, he in eleventh" (p. 316).

Although Jude confronts Zephyr at the end of the novel, teachers can push students to consider how this falls into the category of date rape. Girlshealth.gov (2015) offers definitions and explanations as well as resources for date rape and sexual assault. Students can discuss the consequences of what happened to Jude and imagine how Zephyr could have been held more accountable for his actions.

Furthermore, Noah also experiences a scene in which he is kissed at a party without giving permission; he asks himself after, "Did that really just happen to me? Did I imagine it? Um, don't think so, because I certainly wouldn't have picked her if my imagination were in charge" (p. 125). Both events could lead to a productive conversation with students on the issue of consent, and students could consider: *What does it mean to give consent? What does it look and sound like? What does consent feel like?*

Teachconsent.org (Virginia Sexual and Domestic Violence Action Alliance, 2017) has some helpful resources for helping youth understand and engage with the topic of consent, as does the Wisconsin Coalition Against Sexual Assault (2018). The latter curriculum includes a host of resources divided by target age groups and contains images and videos that illustrate how everyday actions might be complicit in assault, such as not calling out instances when one is privy to details about them (see chapter 7, Women's Rights, for more ideas on teaching about consent).

Teachers may also wish to note for students that "it is no longer acceptable to pretend, as some do, that rape and sexual assault are only committed by men against women . . . male rape victims face an enormous amount of social prejudice in coming forward" (Amherst, 2010, para. 2), or that date rape only occurs by heterosexual individuals. While sensitive issues, these are crucial to bring into conversations so that students will feel knowledgeable and empowered.

After Reading

Once students have completed reading the book, they can engage in reflection on the complicated nature of the characters and relate these to humanity at large. While each character possesses a "good" side, they also demonstrate negative characteristics. For instance, Jude saves Noah from drowning, but she also threw away his application to the art school. Noah loves Brian deeply, but shares his secret openly. Noah and Jude's mother loves them, but she cheats on their father. Students might discuss how the characters are reflective of real people and illustrate the complexity of individuals, contemplating: *To what extent is it possible for one person to be entirely "good" or "bad"? What mistakes are forgivable? Where do you personally draw your lines in terms of betrayal and compassion?*

Readers might also wish to further explore the artwork and various mediums described in the text. Noah catalogues four pastel drawings he imitated from the museum visit with his mother, "a Chagall, a Franz Marc, and two Picassos" (p. 21). Students could examine the works of these artists and speculate which ones Noah might have seen. They could also locate examples of sand sculptures like those Jude created that gained her admission to the art school as well as stone sculptures like the one she is trying to create. They might speculate as to why Jude chooses stone for her sculpture and even what her final product might look like, locating potential examples from their research.

Students could also create graphics to illustrate, supplemented by textual evidence, how Noah and Jude both changed throughout the story. In a way, the two "change places" due to the circumstances they experience. They might consider and research, after documenting these changes, how each coped with their grief and what some other healthy coping strategies could have been.

Students could also choose to narrate different endings to the story, answering, for example: *If Noah's mother had lived, how might things have changed? If Noah had been admitted to the art school with Jude, how would this have gone?* They could write and act out short scenes to illustrate their thoughts. They could also create their own digital book trailers, complete with a cast and theme song, for the book, careful to select from the many plotlines those that they think would be most appealing to a wide audience.

On a somewhat different note, and given Brian's concerns about being gay and playing baseball, students could further explore attitudes toward LGBTQIA+ individuals in sports and what related protections (or limitations) are in place for those individuals. They might also research professional athletes who identify as LGBTQIA+, starting with those who compete in the Olympics, for example (Outsports, 2018), or they could search within a specific sport of their interest. They could then share the stories of those individuals through visual mediums such as collages, videos, or drawings. Students could consider if being gay or lesbian is more accepted in particular sports (e.g., dance, cheer) than others (e.g., baseball), and analyze why that might be the case. They could analyze the systemic structures that have led to differential treatments in sports, both at their own level and in professional realms, and brainstorm ways to dismantle those structures.

IDEAS FOR SOCIAL ACTION

Because the book deals with so many heavy issues, students' social action projects could tackle a host of various topics. They might wish to research and provide resources for students dealing with loss or grief, suicide, divorce, or bullying and place information on school websites, bulletin boards, or other places in their local communities where youth spend time. They could locate and advertise (or create) support groups for any one of these issues or establish a general peer support team in which youth are trained and are available for their peers in times of need. Of course, information about school and professional resources should also be made available and accessible, but peer support, especially by those who have experienced similar situations, can be very helpful for students.

Related to Jude's assault scene and her later relationship with Oscar, students could research laws related to consent and age, which differ by state. They might create a social media campaign or host an awareness night at school to publicize what consent means for their peers and to ensure that youth are informed.

If the students' school does not have a gay-straight alliance or similar support structure, students might seek to find a faculty sponsor and create one. They could also host workshops on being an ally for youth, teachers, parents, and community members and create a video of allies talking about their support to share widely. Students might also research their school policies on bullying, especially as it is related to LGBTQIA+ individuals, and issue recommendations for additional protections for these marginalized populations.

In order to increase visibility in their schools, students might also research famous individuals and leaders who identify as LGBTQIA+ such as Prince, Leo Varadkar, Sally Ride, or Laverne Cox. They could also examine people who are steadfast allies. From either, they could create posters to display throughout the school to document the achievements of those figures. They could also post inspirational quotes from well-known artists, such as lyrics from "Brave" by Sara Bareilles or "Born This Way" by Lady Gaga. They could begin by viewing the documentary *The Out List* (Greenfield-Sanders, McConnell, & Walker, 2013) and identifying people whose stories they want to highlight. They might also include local community members who are out and potentially invite those individuals to their school to speak either about their sexuality or about their occupations, and more. Reducing stigmas around sexual orientations is an achievable goal and one that such actions can empower our students to accomplish.

SUPPLEMENTAL RESOURCES

Canonical Companions

Giovanni's Room by James Baldwin
Maurice by E. M. Forster
The Picture of Dorian Gray by Oscar Wilde

Connected Young Adult Literature

Will Grayson, Will Grayson by John Green and David Levithan
Am I Blue? Coming Out from the Silence edited by Marion Dane Bauer
Openly Straight by Bill Konigsberg
Aristotle and Dante Discover the Secrets of the Universe by Benjamin Alire Sáenz

Connected Music

"Just a Girl" by No Doubt
"Brave" by Sara Bareilles
"Born This Way" by Lady Gaga

REFERENCES

Amherst, M. (2010, March 17). Rape is not just a women's issue. *The Guardian.* Retrieved from https://www.theguardian.com/commentisfree/2010/mar/17/stern-review-male-rape.

Bauer, M. (1994). *Am I blue: Coming out from the silence.* New York: Harper Collins.

Finnegan, C. (2018, October 2). Trump administration halts visas for unmarried same-sex partners of foreign diplomats. *ABC News.* Retrieved from https://abcnews.go.com/Politics/trump-administration-halts-visas-unmarried-sex-partners-foreign/story?id=58222208.

Girlshealth.gov. (2015). What is rape and date rape? Retrieved from https://www.girlshealth.gov/safety/saferelationships/daterape.html.

GLAAD. (2018). GLAAD media reference guide—lesbian/gay/bisexual/queer glossary of terms. Retrieved from https://www.glaad.org/reference/lgbtq.

GLSEN. (2018). New GLSEN national school climate survey. Retrieved from https://www.glsen.org/article/lgbtq-secondary-students-still-face-hostility-school-considerable-improvements-show-progress.

Greenfield-Sanders, T., McConnell, S., & Walker, T. (Producers) & Greenfield-Sanders, T. (Director). (2013). *The out list* [Documentary]. United States: Home Box Office.

Human Rights Campaign. (2018). Growing up LGBT in America: View and share statistics. Retrieved from https://www.hrc.org/youth-report/view-and-share-statistics.

National Center for Transgender Equality. (2018). The discrimination administration: Trump's record of action against transgender people. Retrieved from https://transequality.org/the-discrimination-administration.

Nelson, J. (2014). *I'll give you the sun.* New York: Penguin.

Outsports. (2018, February 14). 2018 Olympics will have a record 15 out LGBTQ athletes. SBNation. Retrieved from https://www.outsports.com/2018/2/6/16924846/2018-winter-olympics-pyeongchang-out-gay-lesbian-bisexual-athletes.

Pieklo, J. M. (2018, June 26). The Supreme Court recognized marriage equality three years ago. Now same sex adoption is in danger. *Rewire News.* Retrieved from https://rewire.news/article/2018/06/26/marriage-equality-same-sex-adoption/.

The Safe Zone Project. (n.d.). Curriculum. Retrieved from https://thesafezoneproject.com/curriculum/.

Virginia Sexual and Domestic Violence Action Alliance. (2017). Teachconsent.org. Retrieved from http://www.teachconsent.org/#new-page.

Wisconsin Coalition Against Sexual Assault. (2018). Retrieved from https://www.wcasa.org.

12

ENVIRONMENTAL PROTECTION AND ECOJUSTICE

Nature writing, environmental (eco-fiction) fiction, ecocriticism, cli-fi (climate fiction), ecojustice—all of these terms relate to writing that is concerned with the environment and humans' interaction with and in it. Ecocriticism has its roots in:

> What would be considered "nature writing"—writers like Thoreau, Whitman, Gary Snyder, and Terry Tempest Williams . . . (and) asks some fundamental questions about the human/nature interface, a zone of interaction which is continually contested: how does the author represent nature in the text? How do humans interact with/perceive nature? What environmental issues are subtly—or not so subtly—portrayed in the text? (Arigo, 2014, p. 115)

Similarly, environmental fiction:

> needs to explicitly assess humanity's impact on nature. Environmental fiction comes in two categories: *what is* and *what might be*. What Is encompasses the present and the past. It tells a story based on observable facts. What Might Be projects those facts into the future. It uses details to teach a lesson, often a cautionary tale, of what might happen if humanity continues on its path of destruction. (Renner, 2017, para. 4)

The term *ecojustice* was first used in 1973 by Norman Faramelli, who defined it as "the simultaneous concern for social justice and environmental quality plus their interrelationships" (cited in Bakken, n.d.). Bakken (n.d.) furthers this explanation, noting:

> "Eco-justice" tends to focus on a certain subset of problems for social ethics—those where questions of social justice and questions of environmental ethics overlap. Such issues include: social, environmental, and resource limits to some forms of economic growth; energy production and the distribution of energy and resources; the exploitation of indigenous lands and peoples; land use, agriculture, and world hunger; population growth; the siting of hazardous industries and waste sites in poor and minority communities; and environmental protection and employment. (para. 3)

Shortly thereafter, in 1975, the term *global warming* was introduced by Wallace Smith Broecker, an oceanographer, which slowly became part of both the sciences and literature connected to the repercussions of humans' impact on Earth (Martin, 2018, para. 1).

Most recently, in the 2000s, the term *cli-fi* (climate fiction) emerged on the literary scene. With obvious connections to the term *sci-fi* (science fiction), cli-fi refers to "any fictional work written about the effects of climate change and global warming" (Martin, 2018, para. 4). These works often take place in futuristic (dystopian) societies where the planet has been all but destroyed due to environmental desecration.

In this chapter we focus on environmental protection in general and ecojustice in particular. These topics are important for students to consider as the world is ever-changing, and they and their future children and grandchildren will have to live with the environment that has been passed down to them from previous generations. A unit of study on ecojustice—integrating science, literature, history, and politics—can help students to identify ways in which they can learn from the past and enact positive change for the future world in which they will live.

THE MARROW THIEVES

The Marrow Thieves, by Cherie Dimaline (2017), takes place in a futuristic society where the environment has been all but destroyed by global warming. People, except for those who are of the North American First Nations,[1] can no longer dream—which has driven them to despair, irrationality, immorality, and the willingness to commit unspeakable acts. Those who can no longer dream believe the cure can be found in the marrow of the Indigenous people, and as such, Recruiters, military agents of the government, have begun hunting and capturing Indigenous people, extracting their marrow for their personal use. Boarding schools like those of the past have been reopened as holding cells and places whereby the marrow extraction is completed.

Sixteen-year-old Frenchie is on the run from the Recruiters. Having been separated from his family, he is taken in by a group of other lone travelers. As the story progresses, the reader learns of each of the group member's "coming-to" stories (how they "came to" be who and where they are today) as well as how they live on the run, trying to preserve their language, culture, humanity, and hope for a better tomorrow. It is a story of survival, strength, resistance, and hope.

We chose this book because not only does it offer readers a vehicle by which to consider the extreme repercussions of destroying the environment but also how desperate people can fall into performing horrific acts in efforts to save themselves. Additionally, *The Marrow Thieves* provides a backdrop by which to explore the history of Indigenous people and the ways in which they have been abused and marginalized in the past, as well as offers space to reflect on the power of the older generation—what can and must be learned from them in order to not repeat the mistakes of our past, how we must fight to protect languages and cultures of Indigenous people that are rapidly disappearing, and our civic responsibility to speak out and up for those from vulnerable populations.

TEACHING STRATEGIES

Before Reading

To begin a study on environmental literature in general, and ecojustice in particular, students will first need to become familiar with various terms (*nature writing, environmental fiction, ecocriticism, cli-fi, ecojustice*). Teachers can lead students in creating definitions for the terms by providing for them examples of different types of writing and encouraging them to try different forms of writing as well. For example, teachers can start with nature writing—sharing some poems of Walt Whitman, Gary Snyder, and Terry Tempest Williams. They can identify the similarities in the poems they read—content, mood, tone, themes. Following, they can go on their own "nature walk" around their school and/or community, taking photos of what they see, jotting field notes of what they observe, and then creating their own nature writing poems, perhaps modeled after the poems they have already read.

Later, students can explore various examples of environmental fiction. Using the definitions they created in the activity mentioned above, students can categorize the works they read and view into the two proposed categories: *what is* and *what might be*. For each poem, song, and/or video analyzed, students can analyze questions like *How is nature portrayed in this piece? How are humans portrayed? What is the relationship between humans and nature? What is the human impact on nature? Should this be changed? How? Why?*

There are a variety of short, animated films that students can view and analyze, focusing on the above-mentioned questions. Wilson's (2008) five-minute animated short, "Human-Nature" (Mudpuppie Design, 2010), offers a look at how we impact nature on a micro level. Similarly, Animal Planet has a series of animated shorts that can be accessed via YouTube called "The Animals Save the Planet."

These short, cute, funny cartoons are all under a minute long and offer information about various ways we can reduce our footprint on the planet, from "Romancing the Bag" (Animal Planet, Romancing, 2008), which shares how plastic bag usage is harming the environment, to "Elephant Shower" (Animal Planet, Elephant, 2008), which focuses on water conservation.

If teachers want to include a feature-length film in order to guide students through a more robust film analysis, they might consider animated films like *The Lorax, Happy Feet, Isle of Dogs, Fern Gully: The Last Rainforest*, or *Bambi*, or nonanimated films like *Avatar, I Heart Huckabees, Chinatown*, and *Erin Brockovich*. Again, they can consider the questions: *How is nature portrayed in this piece? How are humans portrayed? What is the relationship between humans and nature? What is the human impact on nature? Should this be changed? How? Why?*

In all cases, teachers should screen all films before assigning them to ensure that they will meet the learning, social, and emotional needs of their students.

Once students feel comfortable with the concept of ecocriticism, teachers might want to push their understanding even further, with an investigation of what the word *ecojustice* means. The Teaching Tolerance website offers a lesson plan titled "Analyzing Environmental Justice," which contains objectives for assisting students in their understanding of "how pollution disproportionately affects people who are poor and members of racial and ethnic minorities as well as . . . a map to locate environmental injustice" (Teaching Tolerance, 1991–2018, para. 1). Through this lesson, students can begin to discern how issues related to the environment connect with issues of equity as well.

While the focus of this chapter is on ecojustice, it would be remiss to exclude information for helping students understand the significance of the boarding schools that are portrayed in the book *The Marrow Thieves*, and the history of oppression and forced acculturation that surrounds the North America government's relationship with people of the First Nations. The Library of Congress offers lesson plans for introducing students to the American Indian boarding schools of the late 1800s through the mid-1900s.

Through an analysis of primary source documents, including photos, stories, schedules, and articles, students can learn about boarding schools, the recollections and feelings about the schools of students who are survivors of them, and consider why this is not a highlighted feature in typical US history textbooks. In addition to resources, suggested procedures, and evaluation ideas, the lesson plans also include extension activities that might be useful, such as "Investigate past or present attempts of forced assimilation in other cultures" and "Map the locations of American Indian boarding schools in the United States" (Library of Congress, para. 7). These would aid students in applying their knowledge to broader contexts and facilitate their critical readings of their country and perhaps even their own geographic regions.

Despite the fact that the *The Marrow Thieves* takes place in Canada, very similar acculturation attempts were committed in North American countries. Thus, beyond boarding schools, students can make additional connections to the North American government's treatment of Indigenous people as they read, such as examining primary source documents related to treaties and land rights. Students can track and relate these instances to ecojustice violations as they encounter them while reading the book, using textual evidence to support their claims.

During Reading

In *The Marrow Thieves*, the kidnapping of people from the First Nations is instigated by a desire to regain the ability to dream. The book describes the Recruiters as wearing windbreakers with a logo that says, "Government of Canada: Department of Oneirology" (p. 19). Teachers can ask students to guess what *oneirology* means, using word roots before looking up the definition ("the scientific study of dreams") as well as how the study of dreams is and can be used to help people in the world today.

While reading, teachers might also have students consider the importance of remembering and learning from the past. Frenchie's father tells him and his brother that they "were lucky (they) didn't remember how it had been so we had less to mourn" (pp. 23–24). Teachers can ask students their opinion on that sentiment: *What are the benefits to not remembering bad times? What is the danger in not knowing about the past? What are other events in our history that we need to remember in order to not make similar mistakes in the future? How should we remember or pass down information?*

The book describes a futuristic society and the ways in which the destruction of the environment has changed it from the past:

> Here the sidewalks were shot through with arterial cracks and studded with menacing weeds that had evolved to survive torrential rain and the lack of pollinators. Wildlife was limited to buzzards, raccoons the size of huskies, domestic pets left to run feral, and hordes of cockroaches that had regained the ability to fly like their southern cousins. (p. 31)

Teachers can lead students in analyzing these descriptions and investigating the science described. Using what they know about ecology, biology, and evolution, students can determine the plausibility of such an environmental change in the future, perhaps preparing a debate to argue their chosen (or assigned) side.

The protagonist of the novel explains that he "was nicknamed Frenchie as much for my name as for my people—the Metis" (p. 68). One of his travel companions, Miig, is Anishnaabe, "an ethnic term, referring to the shared culture and related languages of the Algonquian tribes of the Great Lakes area" (Native languages of the Americas, 1998–2015, para. 1). Students can research the various Indigenous groups identified in the novel as well as native tribes in their own communities and surrounding areas to learn about both their past and present lives.

In addition to mapping out the locations of various Indigenous communities, students can research the languages and culture of their chosen group, considering questions such as: *Why has the language of many tribes been lost? What is lost along with language? How can language be preserved? What is the value in doing so?*

Also while reading the book, teachers may want to help students continue to explore the portrayals of ecojustice in this cli-fi novel. There are a variety of videos that can help make the concept of ecojustice more accessible to students. For example, the short video "Environmental Justice, Explained" shares, "We already know that pollution and climate change negatively affect people's health and quality of life. But we're not always clear about which people are most exposed and impacted" (Grist, 2016). This video can facilitate students' recognition again of how issues of the environment might interact with social contexts.

Another short video, "A Brief History of Environmental Justice," shares information such as how "landfills, chemical waste facilities and power plants are more often built in poor and minority communities, which don't have the power or money to advocate for themselves" (ProPublica, 2017), and the TEDx talk, "The Great Pacific Garbage Patch" by Van Jones, focuses on how plastic pollution disproportionately affects people who live in poverty (TEDx, 2010). Combined, these videos can help students better understand the systemic nature of ecojustice. Using what they have learned from the short videos, teachers can lead students in identifying specific aspects of the novel that help to categorize it as an ecojustice piece of literature.

The potential for water wars, conflict that is and will continue to arise due to shortages of water, is a real concern for those engaged with global warming issues. There are a variety of resources available that can help students to better understand this concept, both as it is depicted in the novel and as it may occur in the real world in the future.

In *The Marrow Thieves*, Miig describes the water wars:

> America reached up and started sipping on our lakes with a great metal straw. And where were the freshest lakes and the cleanest rivers? On our lands, of course. . . . Too bad the country was busy worrying about how we didn't pay extra tax on Levi's jeans and Kit Kat bars to listen to what we were shouting. The Great Lakes were polluted to muck . . .

they were fenced off, too poisonous for use. . . . The Water Wars raged on, moving north seeking our rivers and bays, and eventually, once our homelands were decimated and the water leeched and the people scattered, they moved on to the towns. Only then were armies formed, soldiers drafted, and bullets fired. (pp. 77–79)

After reading this section of the text, students can watch the documentary *Blue Gold: World Water Wars* (Achbar & Bozzo, 2008). They can write a compare/contrast essay, comparing the water wars as presented in the book and the documentary. They can also write a problem/solution essay or speech to share what they have learned.

Students might also be interested in researching other conflicts regarding natural resources and Indigenous people, like the Dakota Access Pipeline controversy of 2017. The website Cultural Survival (2018) offers many documents and news stories regarding topics of unique consideration for people from Indigenous communities around the world.

After viewing and while reading, students can make connections to the text and also conduct outside research on the topic, investigating other environmental crises and how various marginalized groups are disproportionately affected. Connections can also be made to developing countries, like those mentioned in chapter 6, Refugee Crisis, and chapter 2, Global Poverty.

After Reading

After reading the novel, students can read a short article by the teen who was the cover model for the book about what the book means to him (CBC, 2018) as a part of an underrepresented and often marginalized group. They can also research different organizations that help to support, preserve, and protect the languages, cultures, and lives of Indigenous people around the world, like the Indigenous Education Institute (2018), Cultural Survival (2018), and the Indigenous Peoples Council on Biocolonialism (n.d.).

Focusing on the environment, students might research various organizations in the United States and globally that have missions to protect the environment, like 350.org (n.d.), the Intergovernmental Panel on Climate Change (IPCC, 2018), and the World Wildlife Fund (WWF, 2018). They can choose an aspect of the environment about which they feel most passionate, research it and the ways in which it can be supported, and share the information they find in a poster, report, or speech.

Teachers can lead students in using the text as a vehicle to contemplate the morality of people and the instigations for the choices they make. In *The Marrow Thieves*, Frenchie explains:

> It seemed as though the world had suddenly gone mad. Poisoning your own drinking water, changing the air so much the earth shook and melted and crumbled, harvesting a race for medicine. How? How could this happen? Were they that much different from us? Would we be like them if we'd had a choice? Were they like us enough to let us live? . . . What would I have done to save my parents or Mitch, given the chance? Would I have been able to trap a child, to do what, cut them into pieces? To kill them alive? . . . I didn't want to know what they did. And I didn't really want to know if I'd be capable of doing it. (pp. 143–144)

Within all people is the capacity for good and evil, and history shows us that desperation yields to desperate actions. Students can research other examples in history where desperation yielded desperate actions from individuals and/or groups of people, considering questions such as: *Is this ever OK? Is it understandable? Are some lives worth more than others? Who gets to decide?*

Similarly, Minerva in the novel poses the question, "Do you think circumstances make people turn bad? Or that people make circumstances bad to begin with?" (p. 158). Students can take a stance on this question, developing examples from both history and current events to support their claims, and either write a persuasive essay or debate this issue with classmates, in groups or individually.

For a musical connection to the text, Frenchie describes the music of Pearl Jam as, "It sounds like if grey could make noise" (p. 455). Students can listen to various Pearl Jam songs and analyze what they think Frenchie's description means. They can then identify other artists and the colors they believe the groups represent and why as an activity in the use and analysis of author's tone, style, and mood. To extend the activity, students can choose various artists and their identified colors to relate to other texts that have been read that year, providing explanations for their choices that demonstrate their understanding of the literary works.

Also connected to music, students can explore various singers and songwriters who emphasize the environment and analyze how the environmental concerns described in those songs have changed and evolved throughout the years as well as how different genres of music (e.g., country, pop, techno, folk, rap, metal) have depicted environmental concerns through song.

A quick internet search will bring up a plethora of titles like Joni Mitchell's "Big Yellow Taxi," The Beach Boys' "Don't Go Near the Water," Marvin Gaye's "Mercy, Mercy Me," Michael Jackson's "Earth Song," Bob Dylan's "License to Kill," The Beatles' "Mother Nature's Song," One Republic's "Truth to Power," and Imagine Dragons's "Radioactive." Students can each choose a time period or a genre, explore the music and lyrics related to the environment, and identify patterns and themes, speculating as to why they think those themes exist.

IDEAS FOR SOCIAL ACTION

The book *The Marrow Thieves* offers a plethora of opportunities to engage in social action connected to environmental protection, but it also provides opportunities to take action in preserving voices and stories of the past. As Dimaline writes:

> We needed to remember Story. It was his job to set the memory in perpetuity. He spoke to us every week. Sometimes Story was focused on one area, like the first residential schools: where they were, what happened there, when they closed. Other times he told a hundred years in one long narrative, blunt and without detail . . . treaties . . . earthquakes . . . because it was imperative that we know. He said it was the only way to make the kinds of changes that were necessary to really survive. "A general has to see the whole field to make good strategy. . . . When you're down there fighting, you can't see much past the threat directly in front of you." (pp. 80–82)

Students can consider the power and importance of storytelling. They might, for example, analyze their own history textbooks: *Whose story is told? Whose voice is omitted? Whose voice is silenced?* Teachers can ask students *If you were to write your own "story," what would you include?* Students can then compose their own individual stories, in whatever medium they choose, and collect those into a consolidated classroom story—as a zine, blog, or book.

This class story can then be shared with younger students in the school district, with families, and with members of the community. Students might even take the stories that they write and turn them into scripts to perform. If they identify an organization they want to support, they can charge an admission to their performance and donate the proceeds to their identified cause.

Art and images can also be powerful in helping students not only better understand the impacts of global warming and environmental justice on humanity, but also inspire them to use their own creative talents to enact change. Teachers can have students read the article "18 Green Artists Who Are Making Climate Change and Conservation a Priority" (Brooks, 2017), as well as the article "Using Photography to Combat Climate Change" (Hertog, 2018), and analyze the artwork displayed.

They might then organize their own art show—soliciting various types of artwork (drawing, painting, photography, sculpture, etc.) that portrays environmental themes from people in their school and/or community. Students can interview the artists, advertise, and stage the exhibit. They might identify an organization that supports environmental initiatives, and collect donations at the door to support their chosen cause.

There are a multitude of simple things that students can do to make a positive impact on their communities and to reduce their carbon footprint, from reducing their consumption of plastic, driving less, composting, and using reusable bottles. Teachers can encourage students to inventory their own habits by using the Carbon Footprint Calculator (EPA, 2016) and design and implement ideas for changing any negative habits identified.

Students can identify an area on which they want to focus for environmental work, be it at the local or global level. Perhaps they want to start a school garden, a composting system for the school cafeteria, or a walk/ride or a bike/carpool to school day. They can create public service announcements regarding the need to conserve water, recycle, reduce their use of plastic, or whatever other environmental topic they choose. Students can make plans of action, propose those plans to the school board, and organize events. They can track their progress in reducing their personal and school's carbon footprints on school websites or on large posters in the schools and community.

While some of the other social issues in this book (e.g., human trafficking, police brutality, refugee crisis) may seem overwhelming, environmental protection can start immediately and with small, everyday concerted efforts. Students should be encouraged to take the lead in determining how they can both make choices and encourage others to make choices that can have large impacts on the environmental stability of our world.

SUPPLEMENTAL RESOURCES

Canonical Companions

The MaddAddam Trilogy by Margaret Atwood
The Plague by Camus
Silent Spring by Rachel Carson
The Road by Cormac McCarthy
Walden by Henry David Thoreau

Connected Young Adult Literature

Pitch Dark by Courtney Alameda
The Hunger Games by Suzanne Collins
The Maze Runner by James Dashner
Hoot by Carl Hiaasen
The Uglies by Scott Westerfield

Connected Music

"Don't Go Near the Water" by The Beach Boys
"Mother Nature's Song" by The Beatles
"License to Kill" by Bob Dylan
"Mercy, Mercy Me" by Marvin Gaye
"Radioactive" by Imagine Dragons
"Earth Song" by Michael Jackson
"Big Yellow Taxi" by Joni Mitchell
"Truth to Power" by OneRepublic

Any songs by Pearl Jam

NOTE

1. We use the terms *First Nations* and *Indigenous peoples* interchangeably in this chapter to refer to those identifying as originating from North America. We have capitalized these words to recognize the unique political and cultural relationships between people of the First Nations and their homelands. while recognizing and respecting the tension in such language due to the plurality of tribal affiliations.

REFERENCES

350.org. (n.d.). Retrieved from https://350.org.

Achbar, M. (Producer), & Bozzo, S. (Director). (2008). *Blue gold: World water wars* [Motion picture]. United States: PBS.

Animal Planet. (2008, April 2). The animals save the planet: Elephant shower. Retrieved fromhttps://www.youtube.com/watch?v=h8Ek3v1RBEU&list=PLBBF70602F5268BA0&index=7.

Animal Planet. (2008, April 2). The animals save the planet: Romancing the bag. Retrieved from https://www.youtube.com/watch?v=VzsQwwnqSGo&index=2&list=PLBBF70602F5268BA0.

Arigo, C. (2014). Creating an exo-warrior: Wilderness and identify in the dystopian world of Scott Westerfield's *Uglies* series. In C. Hill (Ed.), *The critical merits of young adult literature* (pp. 115–129). New York: Routledge.

Bakken, P. (n.d.). Freedom, equality, and community in the eco-justice literature. Retrieved from http://www.meadville.edu/files/resources/v1-n2-bakken-freedom-equality-and-community-in-the.pdf.

Brooks, K. (2017, December 6). 18 green artists who are making climate change and conservation a priority. *Huffington Post*. Retrieved from https://www.huffingtonpost.com/2014/07/15/environmental-art_n_5585288.html.

CBC. (2018, March 14). *The Marrow Thieves* cover model Michael Snake shares how the book changed the way he sees himself. Retrieved from https://www.cbc.ca/books/canadareads/the-marrow-thieves-cover-model-michael-snake-shares-how-the-book-changed-the-way-he-sees-himself-1.4573069.

Dimaline, C. (2017). *The marrow thieves*. Toronto, ON: DCB.

Cultural Survival. (2018). Retrieved from https://www.culturalsurvival.org/latest.

Environmental Protection Agency (EPA). (2016). Carbon footprint calculator. Retrieved from https://www3.epa.gov/carbon-footprint-calculator/.

Grist. (2016, January 26). Environmental justice, explained. Retrieved from https://www.youtube.com/watch?v=dREtXUij6_c.

Hertog, M. (2018, September 10). Using photography to combat climate change. Retrieved from https://artistsandclimatechange.com/2018/09/10/using-photography-to-combat-climate-change/.

Indigenous Education Institute. (2018). Retrieved from http://indigenousedu.org.

Indigenous Peoples Council on Biocolonialism. (n.d.). Retrieved from http://www.ipcb.org.

Intergovernmental Panel on Climate Change (IPCC). (2018). Retrieved from http://www.ipcc.ch.

Library of Congress. (n.d.). Indian boarding schools. Retrieved from http://www.loc.gov/teachers/classroommaterials/lessons/indianschools/.

Martin, E. (2018, May 3). What is cli-fi?: A beginner's guide to climate fiction. *Book Riot.* Retrieved from https://bookriot.com/2018/05/03/climate-fiction/.

Mudpuppie Design. (2010). Award winning animated environmental short human-nature. Retrieved from https://www.youtube.com/watch?v=GWLeMftOgts.

Native languages of the Americas. (1998–2015). Anishinabe fact sheet. Retrieved from http://www.bigorrin.org/anishinabe_kids.htm.

ProPublica. (2017, August 4). A brief history of environmental justice. Retrieved from https://www.youtube.com/watch?v=30xLg2HHg8Q.

Renner, R. (2017, June 24). Environmental fiction: A reading list to save the world. Retrieved from https://bookriot.com/2017/06/24/environmental-fiction-reading-list-save-world/.

Teaching Tolerance. (1991–2018). Analyzing environmental justice. Retrieved from https://www.tolerance.org/classroom-resources/tolerance-lessons/analyzing-environmental-justice.

TEDx. (2010, December 16). The great Pacific garbage patch. Retrieved from https://www.youtube.com/watch?v=3WMgNIU_vxQ.

Wilson, C. (2008). Human nature [Video file]. Retrieved from https://www.youtube.com/watch?v=GWLeMftOgts.

World Wildlife Fund (WWF). (2018). Retrieved from https://www.worldwildlife.org.

CONCLUSION

This book offers a host of texts, social problems, and strategies for addressing cultural matters with youth in order to challenge issues of inequity and prompt students toward action. While we foregrounded twelve issues that teachers can address with our selected novels and hoped to provide numerous avenues for discussions, activities, and projects related to those oft-considered controversial topics, we also noted the intersections of each in an attempt to illustrate how systems of oppression are often interwoven. We also hoped to provide students with more nuanced perspectives of individuals and communities.

For instance, while we highlight *The Girl from Aleppo: Nujeen's Escape from War to Freedom* for representing the refugee crisis, the character Nujeen uses a wheelchair, and our areas for analysis with students include accessibility issues for people with disabilities. We focus on *The Marrow Thieves* to feature ecojustice, but the text and our approaches also emphasize the mistreatment of indigenous peoples. *Yaqui Delgado Wants to Kick Your Ass* reflects bullying among teens but also gendered expectations for Latina youths, and in *I'll Give You the Sun* we stress issues related to sexual orientation but also note that consent and date rape are important elements for students to consider and address. These sorts of connections to additional social topics are made in each chapter, and it is crucial to include them when teaching both as a reflection of students' lives as well as for what they can teach readers.

As we addressed each of these social topics, we included numerous external resources such as websites, films, and news articles that educators can draw upon as critical content knowledge (Dyches & Boyd, 2017), or as information from current events that parallels or extends topics in the texts for student engagement and learning. While we do wish to emphasize that we screened all of the resources we suggest, we also want to advise teachers' discretion—only an educator truly knows their own context and students, thus they should be the ones to determine what materials will best relate to their population. Social justice work varies and differs according to environment and what the students within it most need. Finally, while we do not believe in censorship, we do believe in the teacher's ability and power to determine appropriateness. We believe that students are mature and want to discuss difficult topics—and they should be afforded the opportunity to do so in their English classrooms.

We also realize that many students, especially those who are from privileged backgrounds (Swalwell, 2013), may feel upset, frustrated, or even guilty based on the heavy nature of the issues presented by the novels and works we include (Downey, 2005). However, we remind teachers that this discomfort should be a welcomed and expected emotion. As Adichie (2014) notes, "Thinking of changing the status quo is always uncomfortable" (para. 6), and thus we want students to experience a disequilibrium that will hopefully result in shifting their mindsets and commitments. Our focus on social action, essential to this book, is meant to help students move out of a state of paralysis and into doing something to address society. We want students to channel their distress into action.

To that regard, we give many ideas for social action surrounding each text. It is important again to note, however, that social action projects ultimately *must come from the students*. While we have provided ideas for teachers and students, youths designing their own projects will ensure investment and carry through. Furthermore, we caution teachers that these projects take time and should be implemented in steps that are manageable for students and allow the teacher to serve as a guide.

Models such as Epstein's (2014) or Boyd's (2017) can aid educators in leading students through the phases of research, planning, and action. Lastly, we also counsel against the presentation of social action projects as complete resolutions. Students will not be able, for example, to solve police brutality with one undertaking. We do want them, however, to see the successes of their work and to feel that they have begun a cycle of change. We also want them to understand that social change is ongoing and that their projects can open up new possibilities and paths on which to continue. There are many battles and small victories along the way in a fight for broad-based change.

Our ultimate goal is to make the world a better place for all individuals, especially for those who are marginalized because of, for example, their race, financial status, or geographic location. We believe that young adult texts can help students better relate to, understand, and empathize with these groups and draw authentic connections to the systems of oppression that exist in our society. And with these developed understandings, we believe readers can then be prompted to action. Teachers, with the power to select texts, implement pedagogies, and open doors for students to express their agency thus have an immense role in facilitating social change. If we are to create educational environments that challenge students as citizens, disrupt oppression, and create a more equitable society, we must embrace this role. Reading is important. Discussions can be valuable. But reading *for action*—that is something that can empower, inspire, and, ultimately, change the world for the better.

REFERENCES

Adichie, C. N. (2014, October 17). Chimamanda Ngozi Adichie: "I decided to call myself a Happy Feminist." *The Guardian.* Retrieved from https://www.theguardian.com/books/2014/oct/17/chimamanda-ngozi-adichie-extract-we-should-all-be-feminists.

Boyd, A. (2017). *Social justice literacies in the English classroom: Teaching practice in action.* New York: Teachers College Press.

Downey, A. L. (2005). The transformative power of drama: Bringing literature and social justice to life. *English Journal, 95*(1), 33–39.

Dyches, J. & Boyd, A. (2017). Foregrounding equity in teacher education: Toward a model of social justice pedagogical and content knowledge (SJPACK). *Journal of Teacher Education, 68*(5), 476–490.

Epstein, S. E. (2014). *Teaching civic literacy projects: Student engagement with social problems.* New York: Teachers College Press.

Swalwell, K. (2013). *Educating activist allies: Social justice pedagogy with the surburban and urban elite.* New York: Routledge.

INDEX

ABOUT THE AUTHORS

Ashley S. Boyd is associate professor of English education at Washington State University, where she teaches graduate courses on critical and cultural theory and undergraduate courses on English Methods and Young Adult Literature. A former secondary English language arts teacher, Ashley's current scholarship examines practicing teachers' social justice pedagogies and their critical content knowledge; explores how young adult literature is an avenue for cultivating students' critical literacies; and investigates how students select and implement social action projects in both secondary and university classes. Her book, *Social Justice Literacies in the English Classroom: Teaching Practice in Action*, analyzes case studies of practicing English teachers to identify specific pedagogic approaches for advancing equity both inside and outside of the classroom. She has published in the *Journal of Teacher Education, English Journal, Journal of Adolescent & Adult Literacy*, and the *ALAN Review*.

Janine J. Darragh is associate professor of literacy and English as a Second Language at University of Idaho, where she instructs courses in English Methods, Young Adult Literature, and ESL. A National Board Certified former high school English teacher of thirteen years, her research interests are sociocultural and social justice issues in teaching and learning, young literature, and teacher preparation. Her current scholarship centers on supporting teachers of learners who are culturally and linguistically diverse, teachers of refugees, and teachers in rural Nicaraguan schools. She has published in *The ALAN Review, Curriculum In-*

quiry, TESOL Journal, Action in Teacher Education, English Education, and *Teaching and Teacher Education.*